A CONTEMPORARY
CHRISTIAN
PHILOSOPHY
OF RELIGION

A CONTEMPORARY CHRISTIAN PHILOSOPHY OF RELIGION

by James A. Overholser

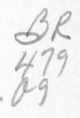

HENRY REGNERY COMPANY
CHICAGO

CONTENTS

PREFACE

THE PURPOSE of this book is to exhibit the primary sources of world meaning. Its development of thought is, in the author's opinion, quite distinct from any comparable discussion to be found in the copious literature now available in the two contiguous fields of the philosophies of history and of religion. A plain indication of the work's aim and scope is given at the outset, in order that the reader may sense clearly what kind of argument he is invited to examine. The relative familiarity of certain basic portions of the material should not induce the reader to a premature impression that he will encounter nothing that is new to him in the researches and results of the central chapters.

Not a few contemporary writers have recognized the pressing need of a new interpretation of the philosophy of religion in our Western World. It is commonly admitted, and can hardly be refuted, that the traditional modes of communicating theological truth are now so ineffective as to mean practically nothing to the majority of cultivated and perceptive people. The philosophy of religion is widely treated either as a matter of quiet irrelevance or as an example of flagrant but innocuous nonsense.

This in itself might not be so definitely alarming, were it not that the more discerning individuals among us have realized that the moral and social values of our civilization are dependent, in some inescapable manner, upon a commonly accepted ground of religio-metaphysical affirmations. A civilization, if it is to endure, must believe in something. If it does not possess a common faith, and the effective motives which such a faith inspires, it is altogether likely to succumb to those who, however scandalous their public faith, believe in something beyond the pale inertia of a purely formal detachment. To be only critical, or to rest forever in the analytic stance, is to persist in apathy. And apathy, in its political aspect, is the dull forerunner of disaster.

The present undertaking is not simply another familiar proposal to reinterpret Christian truth in a modern idiom. It goes deeper. It aims to present a scientific and logical description of the main outlines of a new philosophy of history, of which the pivotal events of the Judaeo-Christian classics, in causal community with the totality of historic occurrence, form the significant core.

In particular, the author has felt, and responded to, the no longer avoidable necessity of coming to terms with naturalism. It is implicit in the present thesis that here, for the first time, a philosopher writing from a generally Christian standpoint has dealt in a fully empirical manner with the central biblical facts without abandoning the historic uniqueness, and primary cultural significance, of Christianity's central figure.

The mood of our world is decidedly and obviously scientific. The essential rightness of the empirical approach, provided the "experience" connoted is sufficiently inclusive, is beyond cavil. The mounting witness of four hundred years authenticates the method; we have, therefore, no option but to think and write, and read and understand, in ways that are in broad agreement with this, the essential character and ethos of our time.

In the development of his theme, the writer has carefully produced an interpretational synthesis of the very divergent philosophies of the two most impressive thinkers in Western philosophy in this century, namely, Martin Heidegger and Alfred North Whitehead. At the same time, a number of other influential movements in current thought have been made to bear effectively upon the task of cultural renewal. The writer shows, moreover, how the metaphysical presuppositions of the past, specifically the assumptions of the so-called Aristotelian substantialism, are now demonstrably infirm and ready for a general replacement. On the positive side, one finds the explanation of new categories of philo-sophical construction, which now are utilized in systematic fashion in place of the outmoded thought-forms. What really occasioned the decline and fall of the ancient theology is told in these pages from a different perspective from that to which most readers are likely to be accustomed.

The heart of the work is an existential interpretation of the personal being of Jesus Christ as understood in reference to an actual and far-reaching complex of historic events. Not least among the original aspects of this volume is the account of what is dynamically involved in "fact," and "meaning," as these and related notions contribute to the shaping of an "historical reason."

It is anticipated that traditional-minded Christians will find the presentation unorthodox and possibly disturbing; and that those opposite ones, the out-and-out positivists, may find it uncongenial because it makes a place for ontological ideas and claims to rehabilitate a large and vital segment of trans-operational religious truth—although in ways that may appear objective to the really open-minded observer.

But among the probable multitude of those who are disposed to be neither orthodox religionists on the one hand, nor undeviating materialists on the other, the point of view of the present reconstruction may prove to be a welcome answer to a most serious and demanding question.

That this independent essay in the cosmology of the two very human and engaging subjects of history and religion may throw some light upon a primordial and indispensable quest is the author's sincere and hopeful wish.

James A. Overholser
Jamestown, North Dakota
January, 1963

1

The Situation of Christianity in the Late Twentieth Century

"Philosophy should now perform its final service. It should seek the insight, dim though it be, to escape the wide wreckage of a race of beings sensitive to values beyond those of mere animal enjoyment."—ALFRED NORTH WHITEHEAD [*Adventures Of Ideas*, p. 204]

THOUGHTFUL observers of life in the second half of the twentieth century can hardly escape the realization that Christianity has suffered a serious decline, and is now in a very tenuous and disturbing relation to the main currents of the modern world. To the mature Christian, who believes that his faith represents a special and invaluable truth for all mankind, this situation is nothing short of alarming. Such an individual is not simply aroused in regard to the security of his particular brand of religion; he feels a keen anxiety, also, as to what may result to our civilization, both in respect of widespread spiritual negation and of actual physical destruction, if this trend is not altered. Our Christian concern is likely to be deepened by the circumstance that a large portion of Christianity's adherents are not even remotely aware of this situation, being misled by superficial appearances to the contrary; and even among those who show some measure of awareness there is a very general failure to understand the real causes of this crisis in the realm of religious faith.

It is time to face more directly and penetratingly than heretofore the question: What is wrong with Christianity in our time? In order to accomplish this we need not only to bring into review a number of factors that are already widely recognized, but also to discover and analyze certain deeper causes which are as yet scarcely heard of, much less evaluated, in their effects upon the whole body of Christian thought and attitude. It is especially important that these latter ideas should be made understandable to intelligent laymen as well as to persons trained in theology; for the thought-life, and possibly the whole future, of every man is involved in these largely hidden, and therefore dangerous, elements of the present situation.

In order to answer the question as to what is wrong with Christianity, we must deal primarily with the Church, because it is to such a major extent the gauge of Christianity's effect and standing in the world. Yet, we cannot simply equate Christianity and the organized Church. The former term we feel must encompass more than the latter, even though there is abundant evidence that the main impulse and principal hope of this religion are in the Church, the confessing fellowship of Christian believers.

As we look at Christianity in our world we are struck first of all with the fact that it is no longer the dominant cultural force that it has been in former periods. It is now plainly a secondary influence, having given place to various secular, materialistic, and humanistic outlooks upon life.

A vivid and telling example is the retrenchment of Christianity before the advances of Communism in many portions of the world. It must be acknowledged that the Communist ideology has shown a far more dynamic influence in many areas than has Christianity. It has produced a spirit of dedication and zeal that has plainly eclipsed the zeal of the Christian enterprise. The movement has been aided by its undeniable success in bringing about social and economic reforms in places where Christian efforts, of all too meager proportions, had barely touched the surface of ancient feudal injustices and corruptions. With a more cogent directness than the Christians of America and other nations of the West, the Communists have managed to promote in some quarters an effective doctrine of the brotherhood of man. Whatever tyrannies and falsities their system may embrace, which indeed are often monstrous, the Marxists gain moral prestige in their opposition to the traditional expressions of social caste and racial prejudice. The failure of our churches in dealing with problems of race is conspicuous. And true democracy is far from universal in the Christian Church.

In general the fervent disciples of Communism have been far more astute in their approach to foreign cultures and psychologies than have the spokesmen of Christianity. All too often Christian missions have failed to understand and appreciate the cultural heritages of the peoples to whom they have come to minister.

Communism, let us observe, is not the only philosophy of life that competes successfully with Christianity in these times. In so-called Christian lands the mood and motives of secularism are so strong as to constitute a definite way of life for the vast majority of the people.

In its ministry to the individual and to the life of the family, Christianity is markedly less successful than in earlier generations. The Gospel is intended to bring release from fear and anxiety, but modern man is more anxious and fear-ridden than perhaps any of his predecessors. Christianity aims at the mutuality of a life of love, yet ours is a society that is so competitive as to be almost unbearable. Christianity preaches individual worth, but ours is an age of dull conformity. Christ exalts the spiritual, while men of today strain increasingly toward the material. He points to life; we seem propelled toward death.

It is increasingly felt by competent students that human

needs in connection with sex and marriage are dealt with today by the agencies and programs of the churches in a way that is extremely inadequate. The course of religion in these areas is often so unrealistic and futile as to undermine all confidence on the part of the persons seeking help.

A large segment of our society gives no thought whatever to religion. The average individual goes from one day of his life to the next without any clear sense of purpose. The world of nuclear fission hangs over him as a vague inhuman threat. Intellectuals assert that ours is an age in which no signs are given. Historians say that we are living in a post-Christian world; that the very expression "Christendom" has long been obsolete. Theologians, even, are not sure of the relevance of the Bible's message to the man of today. The man in the street is, likely as not, a religious illiterate. Yet his illiteracy is not so much the cause, as it is the consequence, of the decreasing stature of Christian truth.

The Church, either in apathy, or in varying degrees of panic in the face of the pressing and seemingly insoluble problems of the current crisis, may be said with some justice to contribute little to the central problems of corporate human life—such as the vexing problems of war and peace, racial and economic conflicts, explosive nationalism, lack of civic responsibility, poverty, educational dilemmas, juvenile crime, degraded popular music and literature, alcoholism, and other social blights. No matter how highly one may esteem the Church or how sincerely one may be devoted to it, one must admit that the Church of the present reveals herself to be, in the words of the hymn writer and to a woeful degree, "unequal to her task." Of course, the Church, as a gathering of human beings, has never been expected to be fully equal to the divine task laid upon her; but, even so, there has hardly been a time when there was so little discernible connection between the Church's spiritual resources, on the one hand, and the most desperate areas of human need on the other. The moral and intellectual instruments by which the truth of the ancient Gospel is to be applied to the complex situations of modern life are painfully lacking.

DIVISION AND CONFUSION

When we contemplate these troubles of contemporary Christianity, we are led to suspect that they are related to the unfortunate, almost innumerable, divisions that now exist within the Church. These are often a source of embarrassment to Christians, not only because the spirit of divisiveness is unchristian, but also because such an extreme fragmentation is a sign of the Church's failure to understand itself. It is, in large part, the lack of a coherent interpretation of Christianity's basic message that produces the seemingly endless disintegration of the movement into sects. This is an unavoidable conclusion, even when we have admitted the emotional and sociological factors which have entered into the formation of the numerous "fringe" denominations that are so noticeable in the religious news of today. With due regard for the sincerity of many of these groups, it can hardly be denied that they give to the public a most unfortunate impression of what Christianity is about—this because of the low cultural level of so many of their activities, and other characteristics revealing their lack of any deep involvement in the history of the Christian Church.

This absurd fragmentation of formal Christianity surely reflects a far-reaching confusion as to what its essential message is. One thing, however, is certain: the questions that exhibit Christian differences today are not limited to the traditional ones of the older denominations, such as, questions concerning (1) the order of salvation, (2) the sacraments, (3) the ministry, and (4) church government. They begin with the nature of God and the vocation of man, if not indeed with implicit questions as to the priority of God or man; but they readily move beyond the conventional formulations. They include, with various others, the following queries: Is it the Church's purpose to enable individuals to go to heaven when they die, or to provide a better life here on earth? Is it to save souls, or to assist the United Fund and the Community Center? Is it by human effort, or by dependence upon God, that the given task is to be accomplished? Is the Gospel a truth in relation to historical truth, or something altogether discontinuous with human and scientific knowledge? Is God a means, or an end? Is religion a life of consecration, or a psychological technique? The articles of Christian faith—are they facts, or symbols? And is the confrontation with Christ a unique event, or does it illustrate a general experience of existential choice? Is this Christian faith institutional, or mystical? Is it individual, or social? Is it permanent, or passing? Is it God's Word to feeble man, or man's feeble word about God?

In view of such ramifications of theological interest (and these questions are undoubtedly an indication of popular theologies that are current) we find that the real divisions are not those of the so-called "denominations," but are rather along the lines of doctrinal emphases that are quite independent of the historic church families. So it is not a matter of one's being a Lutheran, a Calvinist, a Wesleyan, or a Thomist. The real denominations, within Protestant circles, are now: the Fundamentalists, of whom there is so wide a range as to include Billy Graham and Cornelius Van Til on the one hand, and Oral Roberts and Carl McIntire on the other; the Barthians and the Neo-orthodox; the popular Liberals, embracing such divergent types as Norman Vincent Peale and the Moral Rearmament people; the Biblical theologians; the Existentialists; the Confessionalists; the Liturgists; and, one might add, the syncretistic groups, who are making good headway, as may be noted in the instance of

"Unity," Bahá'í, and other exotic patterns. All this adds up, we may reasonably conclude, not to a strength in diversity, but to a weakness in perplexity, and to a grievous scandal in the sphere of our Christian witness. The tragic consequence of this pitiful lack of theological cohesion and clarity is the alarming limitation upon what the churches are doing in the field of religious education and in the interest of a pervasive Christian culture.

ATTEMPTS AT REMEDY

The churches have tried in several ways to increase their effectiveness in shaping contemporary culture. One of the proposals frequently brought forward is that Christians should valiantly return to evangelical orthodoxy. Repeated experience has shown, however, that this is no solution. A stultifying lack of conviction will invariably remain on the part of the freer type of mind; and this sort of theological emphasis is normally marked by a very inadequate provision for applying Christianity to the wider areas of human concern.

A second proposal is the exhortatory demand that Christians should be more completely dedicated. But such a plea, while morally high-sounding, is unrealistic in view of the amount of such exhortation that is already being done. It is merely rhetorical and futile to call for larger dedication unless some more effective insights and motives can be introduced.

A third reaction is to seek greater effectiveness through organization. In this, the churches are nervously aping other groups and institutions without realizing that over-organization is one of the primary spiritual encumbrances of our age. Instead of adding to the strain of a complex and impersonal social order, the church should offer to individuals some relief from it.

Others have felt that if the Church gave itself directly to the ministry of a "social Gospel," it would thereby find strength and healing. This remedy also fails to go deep enough. The Church may discover that it is not at all sure of what it offers to men's social needs, and is not in position to meet them. These particular needs must be seen in the larger perspective of a profound anthropology, and in reference to political realities.

In the fifth place, there is the recurring invitation to come back into the mother-church of Roman Catholicism. Suffice it to say that to men who love freedom, freedom of thought, of aspiration and of action, the freedom that leads to the unconstrained truth, there is in this proposal no very strong allurement.

Finally, there are those serious-minded churchmen who have attached great hopes to the movement for union among the evangelical bodies. They seem to believe that if the many separate branches of the Church could be merged into one harmonious fellowship, there would be for Christianity a new and triumphant era. This hope is not entirely misplaced, and the goal is certainly to be applauded. But the course of ecumenical effort thus far has met with very limited success. This, we believe, for a number of reasons, of which the principal one is that these statesmen of the coming great Church think almost entirely of achieving union from the outside by manipulating and compromising the time-hardened strands of obsolete systems of church doctrine and polity, instead of approaching the problem inwardly and afresh from the standpoint of a new interpretation of the central Christian facts. It is like patching old wineskins, not with new pieces, as in the parable, but with parts of others equally worn. Or, to use another figure, we must hold that those items of theological experience that have been crystalized for centuries, no matter how illustrious they may be in themselves, or how vital they may have been formerly, cannot even by the most potent ecumenical magic be fused into a new ecclesiastical jewel. Only in the original and honest crucible of Christian response, of mind, heart, and soul, in the presence of the primal events, unobscured by the venerable accretions of the centuries, and unprejudiced by selfish fears, can the theology of the ecumenical Church come into being. It will be a new thing, though still the same Body, with the same Head and the same nature, made possible alone by Him who makes all things new.

Over against the foregoing recommendations for alleviating the plight of Christianity in our time, we must put another and different proposal, which has a better likelihood of furnishing the solution of our problem: that is, a theological renewal, a deep, thoroughgoing re-thinking and re-formulating of Christian truth in terms of the thought-forms that are increasingly familiar to intelligent people of our day, and in reference to the actual human and corporate needs that exist in our world.

There exist in our world numerous indications of the direction in which this necessary project of Christian thought should move. Contemporary fields of knowledge provide materials and insights adequate for the task. It is a task requiring both a considerable "wrecking" of archaic structures now standing in the way (though not always visibly!), and, by far the greater part, a positive program for an actual and fruitful communication of Christianity's redemptive truth.

The sort of theological renaissance that is required in our time must, first of all, account for the modern decline of Christian doctrine in ways that go beyond the facts customarily cited in the discussion of this subject. We have heard much, and correctly, about the detrimental effect upon Christian thought of several outstanding scientific developments, namely, the "Copernican revolution" of the sixteenth century; then the Darwinian theory of biological evolution, and the introduction of the "Higher Criticism," both of which had far-reaching and distressing consequences in the nineteenth century. The general effect of these three movements was to destroy the confidence of Christians in a literalistic, absolutist interpretation of Scripture. To these unsettling influences, others somewhat more elusive in respect of their bearing on the popular religious mind, were joined in the radical pronouncements on human nature in the writings of Marx, Schopenhauer, Freud, and other more recent iconoclasts.

THE REAL HINDRANCE

It is exceedingly important to recognize that these developments—vastly influential though they were—do not comprise the most significant force that has gradually brought about the disintegration of the dogmatic tradition and world-view of classical Christianity. The thing that has done most to undermine and generally to negate the conventional form of theology is a thing that goes far deeper and calls for a much more drastic re-orientation. It is the astounding and epochal fact that the basic metaphysic of our Western World has collapsed. This particular metaphysic with its distinctive presuppositions and categories, is now almost completely outmoded as a vehicle of intellectual satisfaction, and is therefore no longer capable of serving as the bearer to our culture of the ultimate affirmations of a Christian world-view.

Let us endeavor now to describe these thought-forms of our Western theological heritage and to see how it has come about that they are no longer adequate for the purposes of a philosophy of religion. It is a matter of where these thought-forms came from, why and how they were appropriated by Christian theologians in the first place, and what it is that has led to the wide rejection of their validity in our time, so that what was once the strength of Christianity has become its greatest weakness.

The normative metaphysic of our Western World is one

whose concepts assume a static, finished universe, whose habit is to treat spiritual realities as though they were natural objects, and whose overall disposition is to separate and departmentalize, essentially to alienate, real entities rather than to conjoin and relate them on the basis of an underlying sympathy. It favors a scheme of things that is atomistic rather than organic—in the long run, a reality that tends to be dead rather than alive. But modern man, quite contrary to this heritage, is growing accustomed to a world that is dynamic, that is marvelously inter-related, that is pulsating with a vital adventure unknown to the ancients. And the twentieth-century observer has, moreover, the feeling of an exciting freedom whose overtones are cosmic. He has, above all, an idea at last by which all things human can be referred to the memory of one supreme Occurrence, and thus be given a richer and more enduring significance. By and large, it is a universe in which far more thrilling paths may be found leading to the eternal. The ancient world-view, with its deification of "substance," of stoic "immutability," is not big enough for it.

The Western ideal of knowledge, which, we maintain, is no longer adequate, had its origin in a singular historic union of Biblical and Greek-Classical elements. If it was the former which provided the content of this knowledge, it was the latter which determined the form. It is with this that we are now concerned.

It came about through the missionary activity of the early Christians, notably in the second and third centuries. As these courageous and impassioned witnesses bore the message of their newfound Christ to the people of the Mediterranean world, they faced an audience whose thought and language were Greek. So, very early, the evangelists became "apologists" as they sought to make the meaning of their Gospel clear to this non-Semitic world. It was a task of translation as surely as it was a mission of proclamation.

The Christians believed that they had a message for all

men everywhere. But when they addressed the Greeks they learned that these men were not particularly interested in the Messiah. They had given no thought to such a matter. They were, however, mightily and consistently interested in the Prime Mover and the Most Real Being. "What is the *One* behind the *many*?" they wanted to know. "And how do you relate what *appears* to what *is*?"

The Christians then proceeded to adjust the Good News of Christ to the monumental metaphysics of the Greeks, thereby connecting with a chain of thought that reached from Thales of Miletus, through the famous schools of Plato and Aristotle, to the jaded Mars' Hill of their generation.

The message came to assume a form like this: God, the Creator, is the Supreme Being, the First Cause, the Most Real Substance, the Explanation of all phenomenal data. Christ, a unique prophetic man of Galilee and Judea, is one with the prior Divine Being. He is the perfect idea, cosmic reason itself, made flesh. The historical Jesus, the man of fulfillment who is the Lord of the Christian believers, is co-substantial with the eternal God. This identity came to be explicitly stated in the great creeds of Christendom. Later theology could speak of a "proper hypostatical union" as being precisely what these creeds intended to define.

The beginning of this process may perhaps be seen in the New Testament itself, in the logos doctrine of the Gospel of St. John, and in certain conceptions of the Apostle Paul which suggest a kinship with terms of Gnostic and other Hellenistic philosophies of religion. Be this as it may, the accommodation of the doctrines of the expanding Church to the forms of Greek thought was timely, psychological, and fruitful. Through this the Gospel was made relevant, and Christian theology became the thought-life, the "perennial philosophy," of the West. By this mode of indoctrination the person of Christ was assured a principle of uniqueness and centrality, and the missionary declaration was given a universal import with intimations of a logical "eternity" that went far beyond the Hebrew "age," or "length of days."

This substance theology, however, which for so long a time has dominated not only the theologian's, but also the common man's views of God, the soul, and divine revelation, was from the beginning fraught with a serious limitation and peril. It tended to objectify God and to rigidify the things of the spirit. In ways subtle, but finally unmistakable, these substantialist categories threw the dull cast of materialism, the character of "thinghood," over the spiritual life they had once successfully fostered.

Especially the idea of God and the idea of the inspiration of Scripture have borne the penalty of the "qualitative" and objective definitions of these articles which were imposed by the traditional metaphysic.

These ancient categories, evidently derived by the Greeks from a simple visual experience of the world of natural objects, have been displaced in our analytical and flexible age by non-Aristotelian modes of thought.

A number of powerful movements in the world of science, philosophy and historical investigation have combined to produce the axial shift away from the classical and medieval thought-forms. These must certainly include nuclear physics and the philosophy interpreting this science, various types of existential philosophy, phenomenology, the schools of analytical and "depth" psychology, the *Gestalt* psychology, the new language-study discipline of semantics, and the "life-philosophies" of Dilthey, Nietzsche, Bergson, and Ortega y Gasset.

Though there are many intelligent readers to whom even the names of some of these developments are not known, there is no mistaking that we are dealing here with potent and inescapable influences which largely determine our cultural climate. They are a part of everyone's experience, whether one is aware of it or not. That their significance can not only be grasped by the thoughtful reader, but also constructively employed by him for the achievement of a renovated and clarified religious outlook, is basic to the present thesis.

In summary, the problem of Christianity today is the need of a more capable and satisfying Christian theology. We want a new and deeper endowment of meaning—not only a sense of individual purpose, but also that which must underlie our personal significance, an impression of a total, visible meaning coming to us steadily from the larger situation surrounding us in time and space. In this time when our most pervasive anxiety is that of the awful threat of unmeaning, we are athirst for that which alone can deeply comfort us, that without which we cannot begin to be whole again, that which is necessary to keep human life human, that is, world meaning.

2

New Instruments of Interpretation

"In other words, the collapse of physical reason leaves the
way clear for vital, historical reason." —JOSÉ ORTEGA Y
GASSET [*Toward a Philosophy of History*, p. 183]

THE revolution of modern science, while rendering many
of the older thought-forms obsolete and useless for the purposes of a serious philosophy of religion, has at the same
time provided new and challenging categories which are now
explicit enough for the task of reconstruction. In this chapter we will describe these and indicate the sources from which
they are derived. They are, on the whole, far more amenable
to the requirements of theology than the substantialist, Aristotelian thought-forms which they have largely displaced.

In particular, the intellectual advances of our time have
given us three basic concepts which have a tremendous potential for communicating the heritage of our biblical faith.
These are: the new concept of *fact* and *event,* the new concept of *meaning,* and the new concept of *being.* Concurrent
with these and in a measure embracing them, is a new and
deeper grasp of the reality of history as both revelatory
medium and spiritual reality. And this, in turn, has occasioned a fresh evaluation of the traditional natural-supernatural dichotomy in relation to the task of Christian scholarship. These are to be dealt with in turn.

First: the new concept of fact and event. To become aware of the striking change in this area one must see what contemporary science has done to the traditional concept of substance. In the light of this development we can note how the concept of fact and occurrence has been radically altered. And it should be borne in mind that substance is the central category of classical science and metaphysics alike.

Modern physics has eliminated the idea of substance even from the realm where it palpably originated, that of visible, material existence. For this nuclear science has learned that a stone, for instance, is not a uniform, homogeneous lump of matter. It is, rather, a grouping of atoms in constant motion, with relatively vast empty spaces, as in a solar system, separating the centers of energy. And the nuclei are not to be thought of as "solid," but in terms of function and of mathematical equations. Thus we are living in a "universe of waves," to use a familiar phrase of Sir James Jeans, a mathematical universe whose creation appears as an act of thought.

What we have regarded as "things" are in reality structures of events, and nothing can be understood except with reference to time. The "field theory" entails that there are no fixed, simple facts in the physical world, no local determination of the kind taken for granted prior to the principle of relativity. We can no longer say of an object that it is simply "there"; the absolute frame of reference is gone. According to Einsteinian physics all possible measurements of time and space necessarily involve our position. The universal instant has existence only in our imagination. We face the tantalizing circumstance that what is earlier *here* is, in a given instant, later *there*. The universe is an infinity of clocks!

The new cosmology, deriving not only from the type of analysis mentioned above but also from the "Principle of Indeterminacy" of Heisenberg, makes a much larger place in scientific thought for the conception of organism. It tends to draw the natural sciences and the study of all historical and psychological subjects into a vital and provocative unity, especially in the masterly interpretation of these implications of physics as found in the writings of the late Harvard philosopher, Alfred North Whitehead. Regarded by many as the greatest metaphysician of this century, and of undoubted competence in the empirical sciences, this profound thinker has created for us the impressive philosophy of organism, in which we have the most complete and cogent interpretation of the world as processive reality. His system is set forth most clearly in his books, *Adventures of Ideas,* and *Process and Reality.*

In the philosophy of Whitehead the physical thing is a certain coordination of spaces and times and of conditions centering in the supposed thing. This center of coordination is variously named "occasion," "concrescence," "event." An "occasion" is regarded as a focal point where universal "essences" intersect. Component phases of reality, known as "aspects," have a tendency to reach patterns of unity in "occasions." As the tendency toward concretion continues, a group of occasions becomes a "society," or social order. The process is ever advancing into the future, adding to itself, and constantly increasing the width of its relevance. Every event is said to have universal relevance, and this term definitely means more than "relation"; a human and social angle is introduced. There is nothing that is merely an inert fact. Every reality promotes feeling, and is felt. Every occasion in this organismic universe has "prehension" for every other, which is the philosopher's way of saying what he states in more familiar language on some of his pages, namely, that there is a "togetherness of things," which draws the whole universe into a profoundly organic unity so extensive as to leave out no events whatever.

The world, asserts Whitehead, has a strong drift toward

meaning. The larger the "occasion" or "society" the more noticeable is the meaning. The whole environment of process, represented by such terms as *participation, community, relatedness, appetition* (which we take to mean vital inclination), *novelty,* and *importance,* suggests the presence of a pervasive meaning, though the author most often uses the word "satisfaction" to indicate this fact. He conceives the ground of concrescence to be God, and does not hesitate to name the deity in this creative role. Not only does he find evidence of God as the ground of processive reality, he goes farther to propose what in his judgment is the special challenge presented by this new world-view to theology. The spirit and language of Whitehead's suggestion at this point must strike intelligent Christians as uniquely thrilling and inspiring. The eminent philosopher writes, "The task of theology is to show how the world is founded on something beyond mere transient fact, and how it issues in something beyond the perishing of occasions."[1]

This almost mystical concern for the attainment of the permanent and the altogether significant in the midst of the transitory world, this exalted desire for an "imperishable society," leads the philosopher to an even more astonishing proposal which he sets before the world of Christian thought. This he expresses in a sentence that is, on the face of it, hardly more than a magnificent hint. Yet the implications of this brief observation are unforgettable when one has realized what Whitehead is saying; for in essence this brief word is the clue to the restoration of theology. While canvassing the possibilities of the world's broadest realms of significance, he writes, "The final problem is to conceive a complete fact."[2]

The aim of the present volume is to show that Christianity's great fact is the "complete fact" toward which the historical process points, and which in positive centrality it emphasizes as the core of the world's meaning. But for the present we must return to the task of clarifying the concept of *fact* as one of the principal categories of the new philosophy.

We have seen that the philosophy of modern physics, primarily formulated by Whitehead, has its key in the concept of an *event* in the space-time continuum. This event is far removed from the traditional notion of a "fact" as something discrete, simple and self-contained, a kind of thing-in-itself which stands or falls in accordance with what could be found in an actual analysis of the heart of this so conceived fact, quite apart from its connections. The concept of a "bare fact," as a wholly objective and unrelated center of occurrence is now quite untenable, and the impression grows that it could never have been more than an unwarranted abstraction. From our present vantage point, we must consider that a fact is not a local thing, in essence, but is on the contrary a relational complex. While it may be seen to have a focus, its reality is extended and is in vital community with other facts. As an electron has a centralized charge which is "here" and yet the electron is inseparable from a mobile and extensive system, so the fact may be located in its focus, yet not truly defined by this location. The focus may be proved to be the least "substantial" of the various phases of the fact in question. This new conception of fact and event is of the very greatest importance to theology, especially to the task of interpreting the crucial events of biblical history.

THE NEW CONCEPT OF MEANING

Until recently it has been quite generally assumed by those laboring in theology that meaning is a thing altogether bound up with discursive logic. This is the very understandable consequence of an academic heritage of rhetoric and logic that is nearly three thousand years old. So Western man has thought of meaning almost entirely in connection with the spoken or written sentence, the logical proposition. In the nature of the case, or to be more exact, within the range of the prevailing categories, this propositional meaning was of a type that magnified definition and intellectual containment rather than any possible achievement of intuition, synthesis or cultural breadth.

Grammatical meaning, though it gives the impression of movement by virtue of its discursive abutment of one proposition against another in a series that may be well-nigh endless, nevertheless is strictly confined in its grasp of real knowledge by its preoccupation with the task of definition, which is a logical process that sets boundaries and is, as if by instinct, exclusive. Its mathematical affinity is with geometry, and its hallmark could well be the circle or the sphere. This traditional logic overlooks the recurring necessity of new and wider perceptions, and becomes a thing apart from the object it seeks to understand.

Opposed to this is the concept of meaning suggested by the organismic view of the world discussed in the previous section of this chapter. It is based, not upon the mathematics of containment, but upon the theories of structure and function, interrelatedness and vital tendency, that are characteristic of a processive view of the universe.

Our clue to the recognition of a translogical type of meaning is the simple *sign*, which appears in countless varieties. The word *sign* is, of course, the root word of the term *significance*, and it proves, upon examination, to be the very epitome of meaning. Essentially non-verbal (though words are without exception signs) the common sign is in fact the most condensed and vivid form of meaning. Theoretically, any situation, judgment, or function may be telescoped and packaged into relatively simple, unitary items capable of representing the larger entity or field.

Meaning in any of its modes is primarily the conscious appropriation of form, this being the resultant manner in which the human subject senses a group of relations. To be significant is to exhibit relations that are not casual but rather outstanding in the possession of form, and therefore "noticeable." The wider the field of perception the more important, the more truly significant, are the objects grasped.

Because it is representative in character, meaning normally emerges from a situation that points beyond itself. Similarly it indicates possibility. Almost as definitely it necessitates the thought of motion, even if the motion implied is no more than the movement of consciousness from the given sign to the intended goal beyond it. So potent is the sense of direction that rises from the meaningful situation. And this fact of direction is in major opposition to the narrow and static disposition of the meanings associated with traditional logic and epistemology.

Ordinarily the forms in which meaning is grounded are too fractional to have much worth, except in so far as they draw the mind toward larger relational groupings. The more we approach the totality of human experience, which is to say the more we sense the shape of history, the more satisfaction we derive from our experience of meaning. Meaning is the expression of wholeness as opposed to fragmentariness. The most valuable meaning, accordingly, is historical meaning. And it is not the product of verbalization, or even of reason in the Aristotelian sense. It springs from the intuition of historical form.

MEANING AND TIME

Further description of this modern concept of the operation of meaning is made possible by the insights of two powerful twentieth-century thinkers, selected for our present purpose from a much larger company which could be cited. These are the famous French philosopher, Henri Bergson, and the equally incisive Spanish writer, José Ortega y Gasset. Both of these philosophers emphasize in very original and compelling fashion the part which time plays in the constitution of human experience and correspondingly in our grasp of the meaning which this experience conveys. Both of them add impressively to the stature of history and the historical categories as the *sine qua non* of humanistic knowledge and likewise of a realistic procedure in any branch of philosophy.

Henri Bergson, the author of *Creative Evolution*, places great stress upon intuition as opposed to the speculative or discursive reason, and sees all life as an experience within time. Life is duration, and any method of logic or theory of knowledge which ignores the time-factor vitiates the nature of the real. The ordinary logical concept is not a true image of any actual object or experience, but is on the contrary the rudest semblance, lifeless and distorted, of the ever elusive instant. The concept is a static cross section, as it were, of a vital reality that is in continual motion, and whose truth cannot be sliced off and exhibited in this candid camera fashion. The effect of this point of view is to implement very forcefully the concept of meaning which this chapter seeks to interpret. The true nature of any organism is not to be found in an abstract instant, but can only be sensed in the observer's response to the total history of the constantly changing organism. Duration tells the authentic story, and the formal equivalent of duration is time. Vital knowledge must be intuitive, and the material for it is cumulative form. Only when the story is concluded is the character definite. Then it is the memory of the whole process.

A distinct group of modern thinkers related to the vitalist theories of Bergson and Whitehead is that referred to under the designation *Lebensphilosophie*. The foremost representatives of this trend of thought in the nineteenth century were the German philosophers Wilhelm Dilthey and Friedrich Nietzsche. Largely influenced by them in our own century was the scintillating Spanish thinker, Ortega y Gasset. Active until the time of his death only a few years ago, Ortega systematically portrays the historical as affording the truest approach to any subject. He asserts that any particular thing is, above all, the series of conditions which have brought it about. To know anything, one must have been present with it in one way or another from its beginning. Human life, he maintains, is not a "thing," and is not to be thought of as having a nature. What one has is a *history*. That is the primary meaning of any life. In this vein and with massive vision Ortega has developed (in his book, *Toward a Philosophy of History*) the basic orientations of a new type of reason, which he terms *vital* or *historical* reason. The direction of his thought unmistakably coincides with that of the other seminal minds toward whom we have looked for the foundations of a new method of knowledge to be employed within the sphere of historical religion.

Brief consideration should be given also to the bearing upon our task of certain other contemporary intellectual movements which similarly lend themselves as instruments of a new theological method. Principally they serve to confirm the more notable contributions already introduced. One of these subsidiary subjects is the movement known as Gestalt Psychology. According to this concept, fully supported by laboratory tests, the whole of any object, situation, or entity is more than the sum of its parts. The parts have their specific value only in the unique configuration that is constituted by the whole. This total pattern (*Gestalt*) cannot be broken down into its elements without loss of meaning. As a musical piece is more than the sum of its individual notes, the *Gestalt* is more than the sum of its elements.

This psychological concept has strong potential for the new theory of knowledge. It attaches primary importance to the immediate impression of *form* which precedes logical analysis. This principle that the whole is more than the sum of its parts is quite contrary to ordinary logic. According to the *Gestalt* view, knowledge does not come in discrete bits but in an intuited pattern. An illustration known to all students of psychology is that of the experiment in which an ape in a cage "sees" the way to assemble the objects at hand in order to reach the desired banana. From unorganized items he perceives the appropriate and successful pattern. And the principle holds true on levels of experience far removed from Koffka's and Koehler's vivid experiments with animals.

The perceived situation makes sense when its interdependent factors are seen in the living relation. Experience comes, not haphazard, but organized. Knowledge is primarily perception, and its central act is an instantaneous and decisive recognition. Knowledge is not of chaotic materials but of true data, *i.e.*, given meaning. Such a concept demands application to the incomparable wealth of historical information, above all to history's most central occurrences, which, we will attempt to show, have to do with the actions of the living God in history.

There is yet another current and very influential movement affecting the philosophy of religion. It is the type of philosophic outlook called Phenomenology. Formulated by Edmund Husserl, Max Scheler and other European leaders of the nineteen-twenties, this view holds that knowledge is really concerned with what "appears." The interest of the philosophical inquirer is not in some ultimate "thing-in-itself," which is thought by the phenomenologists to be a fiction, or at least to be problematical, but with the precise structure presented to our consciousness. The implications of this method, all too briefly pictured here, can be seen in reference to the intuitive-historical principle of knowledge. Its relevance to the philosophy of religion will be indicated in later portions of this study.

If space permitted, it could be shown that numerous other modern thinkers, such as Ernst Cassirer, with his philosophy of symbols, and Filmer S. C. Northrop with his concept of the "aesthetic component" in the employ of cultural apprehension, add remarkable weight to the method we are developing in reference to the derivation of meaning from historical experience.

THE NEW CONCEPT OF BEING

It is primarily to the philosophy of existence, clearly enunciated first by the Danish thinker Søren Kierkegaard, 1813-1855, that we owe the new concept of being. This profound and highly original poet-philosopher set himself to oppose the reigning Hegelianism of his day; thus over against the enthronement of the rational ideal, he advocated the concrete reality of individual human experience, particularly that which has to do with personal anxiety, stress, and crisis. In place of the supremacy of general truth, which despite its grandiose claims he saw as sterile abstraction, he established as no writer before him the centrality of the subjective as the focus of actual being.

In the thought of Kierkegaard life is conditioned by time and calls for decision. In the midst of appalling insecurity giving rise to existential dread, the individual finds no real answer in the elaborate testimonies of reason, and, continuing to be aware of painful ambiguity and emptiness must at length take the "leap" of faith. And in this crisis-formed decision the individual becomes an authentic person. His integrity is established as he "produces" himself through this anguished choice. There is a definite logic of this act in which the person is the "construct" of, or "becomes" himself through, his total decision. It is based upon the recognition that choice is the most characteristic existential category. It is the movement of the soul in the consciousness of a desperate, enforced freedom. Every decision, because it confronts the future and is therefore grounded in uncertainty, involves the assumption of a risk. In this crucial moment the eternal is said to be realized in time, and the personality is essentially altered. When this occurs, one chooses oneself, Kierkegaard affirms, in his eternal validity.

When it is shown that "existence precedes essence," as most of the existential writers agree, the focus of philosophic concern is shifted from the objective world of "science" to the human experience which is now seen to constitute real being. Being is no longer basically "something out there." It is the directly known inner life newly ontologized (*i.e.*, given being-status), so that outward things are relatively diminished in their reality, and their associated categories have thereby lost their age-old philosophical dominion.

The two ablest follows of Kierkegaard in the twentieth century are Martin Heidegger and Karl Jaspers. Of the two, Heidegger is the more systematic (though the founder of this movement strikingly maintained that existential truths could not be made into a system) and gives the most definitive account of this mode of thought. Using as his material the insights and moods of Kierkegaard he appropriates the method of his philosophy teacher Edmund Husserl and presents as the result of the conjunction of these two lines of thought (Kierkegaard and Husserl) a thoroughgoing ontology of existence. Through Heidegger's influence more than through that of any other of its exponents, the philosophy of existence has given priority to *human being* and the special thought-forms which explicate it and relate it to every other conceivable branch of knowledge.

Building solidly upon the Danish master, Heidegger shows that man is always infinitely more than what he is at any given moment. He "projects" himself constantly into the plastic future, and so makes himself what he has not been. This idea of the new determination of one's nature through a total choice envisaging the whole past and the whole unknown future is one which has the most challenging implications for the metaphysics of personality and especially for an application to Christological problems.

Comparable existential insights of great value to the study of religion are found in the work of Professor Karl Jaspers. He writes in a very special manner about the individual experience of the "boundary-situations," such as temptation, guilt, loneliness, and the fear of death. These are conceived to be at the edge of finite experience. The characteristic analysis of life at such a critical extremity is in terms of a psychic "shipwreck" (*Scheitern*); yet this may be the moment at which the individual comes into touch with "transcendence," and is "given to oneself" through contact with superhuman reality. Jaspers indicates that the act of existence bears the same subject-object relation to transcendence (God) that the perceiving consciousness bears to visible objects and that the reflective mind bears to ideas. Truth resides in existence as the act of faith. As there is a logical truth, so there is an existential truth subject to entirely different laws. So does Jaspers view the existential experience of modern man as pointing beyond the temporal. We are justified in the inference from his position, that the knowledge of God is not confined to the roundabout knowledge of logic, but is given primarily in the concreteness of the soul's direct perception.

The most penetrating of contemporary thinkers now hold that being is personal, and that the being of any individual is commensurate with his personal action. His deed is the index of his true essence; his being is the correlate and construct of his authentic deed. And this being is superior to, and unassailable by, the object-world without. It is not substantial but historical and must be grasped by the categories of existence.

THE IMPORTANCE OF HISTORY

The foregoing discussion points constantly to the importance of history as the essential climate and mentor of theological interpretation. This position will now be made more explicit.

To recognize the peculiar and superior value of the organic total is *ipso facto*, to attribute importance to history. No *whole*, of human significance, can be realized apart from history. No philosophy of world-interpretation—certainly no realistic theology—can dispense with it. Modern science broadly supports the conviction that the "historical" is by its nature not merely phenomenal, but as Nicholas Berdyaev contends, "deeply ontological."[3]

A full appreciation of history demands, first of all, a recognition of the actual community and vital interconnection between the physical or "natural," and the human and spiritual realms. It also necessitates the treatment of secular and biblical history as related parts of one whole. Fortunately the categories of an organismic world-view make this unitary approach possible and feasible. The concept of event, which is *par excellence* the historical category, is equally well suited to the objective interests of nature and science, and to those psychological and spiritual concerns which are the territory of religion. It goes with process and with existence. It is essential both to the "sacred" and to the "secular." Far from being a party to any conflict of science and religion, this concept demonstrates their actual consanguinity. Religion is thus freed from dogmatic and futile abstraction; while science is delivered from a barren and inhuman autonomy. The relation of the sacred to other history and knowledge is not the dialectical relation of the two sides of a fence, but the vital and indispensable relation of the other bodily organs to the heart. The question is not whether Christianity is unique.

Reputable scientists of our day inform us that everything is unique! The question is, rather, does Christianity's particular uniqueness afford a pivotal redemptive meaning that the world so sorely needs? Does it actually reveal itself as a truth so central and so majestically dominant as to provide the ground of an unmistakable significance?

We shall indeed be happy if the Christian record, the witness of the world's great central, illuminating story and the one "complete fact," can so infuse the natural with the supernatural at every point, that all nature can be seen as the inclusive stage of an illimitable divine drama. The living God is the Lord of history. The God of all nature, who is the ultimate concept, is the inspiration as well as the boundary of science, the necessity as well as the fulfillment of faith.

The historical philosophy of religion must proceed with the courageous assurance that this world is not a theological desert, or a cosmic slum, but the legitimate and "good" creation of the God who is Father of the Lord Jesus Christ.

But there is yet another obstacle in the way of a Christian hermeneutic. It must be recognized and removed. It is the conventional, and too largely unquestioned, theological distinction between the natural and the supernatural. The habit of assuming a thoroughgoing, qualitative differentiation of these broad concepts as absolute opposites is one of the saddest encumbrances that man has ever imposed upon his mental and spiritual life. Of the several unfortunate aspects of the classical legacy, this categorical straightjacket has probably been the most inhibiting and blinding, and there are yet many who find it impossible to cast off the unnatural burden.

The bifurcation of the world into the *natural* and the *supernatural*, for all its intention to reflect honor upon the Lord of history, in reality has the opposite effect of implying a dead, mechanistic autonomy of the major reaches of the cosmos and is much too close to the sterile deism of the eighteenth century to be friendly either to a Christian view of history or to a vital concept of being. If it is to be retained at all, in a modern world-view, it must be radically shorn of its substantialist trappings and made subject to a relational and organic view of history. It must indeed become figurative language except in so far as the term supernatural may be applied to that which is the ground of all being. Another product of archaic categorical abstraction, these terms seek to compress the living, turbulent fulness of a dynamic universe into the rigid confines of inept and soulless conceptual classes.

It is, in effect, a distinction that is more epistemological than real, even within the limits of its own presuppositions. For its habit is to define as *natural* what it thinks it understands, and to call *supernatural* what it cannot explain. On the natural side the idea encompasses a reality that is often far from explicable in terms of "natural laws," and on the other hand the so-called supernatural is quite evidently in active touch with the normal processes of history. We can neither think of the natural as a sphere in which God does not operate, nor of the supernatural as one in which He acts with an arbitrary and isolationist attitude toward His world. Thus the natural-supernatural antithesis appears to be more relative than its absolutist name suggests. It is in the main, unhistorical, unrealistic, and unhealthy. Strictly speaking, the only supernatural is God. When He enters into the texture of this world's experience He has a way of becoming natural. Witness, preeminently, the Incarnation. But in so doing He does not lose His divinity, and the natural reaps infinite gain.

Nothing is simply natural—nothing is wholly supernatural —in a world that bears in all its parts, from the lowliest to the most excellent, the stamp of a divine creation.

One of the prime necessities of the new philosophic outlook is a Christian naturalism. It must be such as to combine positively the ideas of "nature" and creation, of normative behavior and redemptive purpose, of organism and grace. The faith of Israel did not despise the physical world, but saw God in nature, and meaning in history everywhere. The concept of creation acknowledges both the rational and the transrational elements in life. History itself presents the marvelous aspect of a sequence of creative moments. There is no Christian reason why God may not be thought of as still active in creation. If He created only in the past, we are faced with the intolerable notion that the living God is one who *used* to be a creator, but who for some reason has now ceased to be.

Nor is there any difficulty, in the environment of modern science, in our thinking of the existence of extra-empirical elements, which (as in Whitehead) provide the ground of the world's actual concretion. Let these be "supernatural" if you will. They are the presence of God in the heart of each world event. This means, for science, that it must recognize the existence of certain depths of experience which resist a clear and orderly interpretation. There are sudden breaks and unfathomable declivities in this tissue of actuality, as well as broad vistas and alluring procedures. The world is apparently a real continuum, but it is not a simple one.

The persistence of the unknown and the intrinsically mysterious is an ever forceful reminder of the indispensable factor of faith. The knowledge of the world and of God can be completed only in this mode. Reason, rightly understood, is the propaedeutic of faith, the recommendation of the sublime hypothesis. We believe in order that we may understand, for there is no absolute knowledge on our part. And we seek to understand, in order that our belief may stand secure in the presence of real knowledge.

3

The Location of Meaning

"The fundamental principle for the pursuit of this religion is history . . ."—AUGUSTINE [*De Vera Religione* 7:13]

THE world's "complete fact," evoked in concept by the challenging process philosophy of Whitehead, is the great Christian fact which is centered in the person and work of Jesus Christ.

In order to confirm with some measure of cogency this momentous equation of historical fact, it is necessary at the outset to indicate the several requisites, or peculiar qualifications, which must be thoroughly tested, if it is to emerge as the unmistakable center and source of the world's meaning. Manifestly, these characteristics must all be found to be present, and in the highest degree, if the thesis is to be maintained.

On the basis of the formulation of specific categories by the leading exponents of the organismic world-view, and by inferential adaptation of their points of view to the requirements of historical analysis, we are confronted with the following requisites. They are not necessarily exhaustive and they do not, of course, represent the only possible terms in which these categories may be described, but they are sufficiently inclusive to warrant the definiteness of our results. At the same time, they appear in each instance to correspond to valid and appropriate aspects of the subject concerned, that is, the real constitution of the world's pivotal and dominant fact.

These criteria are: actual comprehensiveness; dimensional variegation, or complexity (which is an aspect of structure); distinctive focus (which is also an aspect of structure); inter-relational tension, or dynamic thrust; the presence of a creative community of extra-empirical and natural factors; the emergence of novelty; the quality of enduringness; universal relevance affording unlimited perspective; and finally, as an element which is at once constitutive of all the others, and expressive of the human consequence of the other categories —the emergence of meaning. These criteria, though perhaps sounding very abstract when simply listed here, will be seen to account, in a fully practical manner, for the concrete realities of world history. They will show that the biblical community of events holds a position of historical importance that is so towering as to grant it an unmistakable primacy in respect of world-meaning.

COMPREHENSIVENESS

This first characteristic is one that comes immediately into view and is elementary in regard to our task. It is the visible scope of Christianity as a cultural phenomenon. The point is simply to affirm that the community of facts called Christianity is, significantly, of the very largest magnitude and justifies the claim that it surpasses any other cultural system in actual extent and influence. The claim becomes the more indisputable when one considers that the Christian community of fact embraces not only its own specific institutions (churches, schools, missions, etc.) which assure recognition because of their names, administrative functions and various obvious and tributary connections, but also other groupings, of enormous importance, which are often not recognized as belonging to the Christian culture-system, but which in fact are participants in the overall community as it is identified by its unique foundational events, which are the motivating sources of the several related subcultures. From this overall standpoint the biblical community contains, along with Christianity and Judaism, the extensive Islamic culture and a number of fusions of Christian motifs with Asian religious movements, not to mention the numerous ethical and humanitarian societies in the West which receive their inspiration from Christian teachings.

The Christian churches have a total constituency which amounts to approximately one-third of the human race. These bodies, together with the Moslem culture, make up nearly one-half of the world's population, a bloc in comparison with which the nearest competitors, Hinduism and the Chinese faiths, are a distinct minority. This does not take into account the adherents of world-Communism, which we will interpret in a different context.

What has been said is sufficient to show that on the basis of cultural comprehensiveness the Christian fact is in the position of preeminence. This circumstance alone would be far from decisive in a contest of ideological truth, but it is significant and it opens the door to the more serious stages of our investigation. While it is conceivable that the world's central occurrence might lack this broad public scope in its earliest stages, it is not admissible that such a potential fact could remain "provincial" over a relatively long period of time.

DIMENSIONAL VARIEGATION

What is more pertinent than cultural scope is the dimensional variegation, or unique complexity, which the Christian fact-community presents. This is to be seen in the occurrence of a number of definable dimensions which clearly demarcate the Christian sequence from others. Other religious and cultural histories are sequential in nature, which is to say that they present to the observer a series of facts and developments, which suggests the concept of a single dimension. The series will constantly exhibit the type of connections that are all too glibly described as "cause and effect," and is not altogether unimaginative, but the entire course of the culture's progress is in the line of its appropriate logic. The evolution of doctrine is canalized and of such a nature that it does not introduce striking juxtapositions of widely separate orders of thought. We find that the logic of Christianity, on the contrary, does present extra dimensions. And these are not simply fortuitous; they are impressively cumulative and they reveal the astonishing versatility of biblical truth. Following are four examples of these dimensional situations.

First, there is the remarkable conjunction of the personality of Christ and the moral principles of Christianity. This is not to suggest that there is not always a connection between the personality of a religious founder, *e.g.*, Gautama Buddha, and the continuing body of doctrine associated with his name. Such a connection is, of course, normal. Yet it is a fact that the teachings of Buddhism would continue to be as valid if it were shown that the Buddha never existed. For they consist of a sort of self-sufficient wisdom. The same is true of the doctrines of Lao-tse and of Confucius. But in the case of Jesus Christ, the supposition of His personal reality is a necessary constituent of all but the most marginal teachings associated with His name. Every ethical stance of Christianity is thoroughly and unalterably theological in its essence. It is a two-dimensional ethic, not just in the ordinary sense that every moral principle implies the existence of God, but in the immediate sense that the ethical directive of the Christian is the awareness of the personal demand of Christ.

This inseparability of personal fact and moral principle is wholly distinctive of Christianity. The difference indicated is one of structure and is important.

The second instance of dimensional variation is the tremendous difference which is found between the biblical community and all prior world-views in regard to the concept of *time* and in regard to its actual experience as a mode of existence and knowledge. To put the truth more accurately, we speak here not simply of the Bible-religion's *experience* of time, but rather of its creation of this category as the mode of historical existence.

As interpreted by Tillich, Cullman and other Christian thinkers, the emergence of a sense of *direction* in history and the resultant awareness of time, is a phase of biblical scholarship that is now given rightful prominence. It means that Jesus Christ provides the center of history and thus sets the whole in motion. Prophecy and messianic longing point toward Him through all the pages of the Old Testament; and in the New, the centuries that follow His Incarnation look backward to that same event, while looking forward also to the second and ultimate pole of His coming, thus giving to history its effective framework wherein all lesser happenings have their place. This is in marked contrast to the cyclic and therefore static conception of history held by the Gnostics, Greeks, Neo-Platonists, *etc.*, and as we see it in general in the literature and philosophy of the ancient world. It is only by virtue of the movement which is posited in time by the events of the Bible that history, as distinguished from bare mathematical sequence, comes into existence. Only when there is one occurrence which is truly "once and for all," is there the possibility of a serious evaluation of any single event or sequence. This is a second example of the peculiar structure belonging to the Christian world-view.

The third example of dimensional variation is the unparalleled coincidence of objective and subjective elements found in the contemplation of the death of Christ. Analysis, in so far as it is able to proceed here, reveals first of all the quite unexpected fact that there is a blending of three totally separate motifs for His sacrifice, *viz.* (1) His suffering on behalf of (and in the role of!) the *"righteous remnant"* of Israel —a thing deeply involved in biblical eschatology, (2) His dying for the sake of the immediate political expediencies of the Jewish nation, as seen by the High Priest (St. John 11:50), and (3) the ultimate intention of the Divine Sufferer for the salvation of all mankind. These observations, however, are but preliminary to the fact of the extraordinary correspondence between the death of Christ, as an objective historical and theological fact, on the one hand, and the religious experience of an individual person as subjective reality, on the other. There is a point here, the most crucial point normally in one's personal history, at which the spiritual constitution of man and the historic atonement of Christ coincide in a manner not duplicated in any other area of the relationship of the psychological to objective occurrence. Personal experience and objective history meet redemptively at this one point, which on the subjective side is called variously conversion, spiritual rebirth, religious integration, and which on the outward side is located at a specific juncture in history and is the cross of Christ. How does it come about that there is this complete correlation of two such different species of experience? Why is it, let us say, that relatively immature Christians have often had reason to be confused in this central fact of their spiritual life and have found themselves wondering whether their experience of Christ is essentially a matter of personal psychology or a grasp of something quite outside them in the constitution of the world? It is because, as Tertullian expressed it, "the soul is naturally Christian." For man's spiritual existence the fact of Christ has an objectivity similar to that which the sun has for his light and warmth. The reality of Christ suits the nature and responds to the need of the individual heart with a directness which could not plausibly be viewed in any other light than that of the singular comprehensiveness of the Christian event.

A fourth illustration of the dimensional character of biblical occurrence is to be found in the fact that the center of history, which is the Person of Christ, is the point at which the plane of ordinary occurrence is transected by the vertical of divine being. That this dimension is not a mere abstraction but a real existent within the structure of history, that the world here has unique "depth," will be the main thesis of Chapter VI, in which we will present the outline of an existential Christology. For the present, let us assert without argument that the most compelling instance of the extra-dimensional truth of Christianity is in the classic affirmation that Jesus Christ is at once man and God! *Quod est demonstrandum.* Nothwithstanding, the unique complexity of the Christian event, as a sign of its richer endowment of cosmic significance, is in itself evidence enough.

THE FOCUS OF THE BIBLICAL STRUCTURE

Our response to the biblical structure of events is facilitated by the vivid impression of *focus* which we have in our perception of the overall community.

The focal movement of biblical history is not difficult to determine, and may be sketched as follows; though it should be pointed out that this scheme is historical, in the ordinary sense, only in part. The earlier stages, while historical in the more penetrating sense of the creative fusion of actual and reflective elements, are probably best understood as a profoundly spiritual retrospection from the standpoint of the later experience of Israel at a time when the record of God's dealings with His people had advanced beyond bold questioning to the testimony of a sure confidence.

The subject in the beginning is the whole creation dominated by the human race viewed as one entity. At the time of the Flood described in *Genesis* a judgment is executed upon the race, which has the effect of narrowing it to one family, which will continue, however, to manifest the character of the whole race, but under the conditioning of a second judgment upon sin in the form of a world catastrophe. Within this reconstituted race one particular people are chosen, the family of Abraham, who will become the covenant people of Israel through whom a great redemptive program will be launched. As God's activity in history centers in them, over a period of centuries, and through many vicissitudes, there comes a time when He will deal in a deliberate and special manner with only a fraction of this nation, who are the *"righteous remnant,"* a group intended to be especially useful to Him in His redemptive purpose. Ultimately the divine purpose is narrowed and intensified until it is represented by one single individual, Jesus Christ.

In graphic and summary language St. Paul interprets God's central purpose in history: "That in the dispensation of the fulness of times he might gather together in one all things in Christ, both which are in heaven, and which are on earth . . ."[1] This gathering together "in one," as a vividly focal process, is brought out even more pointedly in the Greek original of this term. The verb *anakephalaiōsasthai* in its root significance means "to bring to a head." Historical tendency comes to a unique intersection at this point. The Greek may be literally represented by "that He might *head up* all things in Christ." The conception is most significant for the philosophy of history, because of the singular pattern implied in this construction of world events.

It is not suggested that only the history which is within this sphere has meaning, but rather that this series forms the inner structure of the whole. "The Bible always assumes," C. H. Dodd reminds us, "that the meaning of this inner core is the ultimate meaning of all history, since God is the Maker and

Ruler of all mankind, who created all things for Himself and redeemed the world to Himself."[2] All history, then, in the last resort is in a sense sacred history.

Having dealt here with the focal aspect of the Christian world process, culminating in one unique individual and proceeding in turn from the same personal center, we need to consider now the dynamic tension which characterizes this process.

DYNAMIC TENDENCY

The data available for an examination of the *dynamic* character of this process are abundant and are ready for at least a beginning of methodical arrangement. Let us now look to some of the biblical facts which illustrate this category. It should be borne in mind that the focal and structural idea is constantly implied in the dynamic.

The knowledge of God and of His righteousness, in the sense of an effective historical force, has a concrete beginning and may be traced to a particular place and people. "He made known his ways unto Moses, his acts unto the children of Israel."[3] The dominant opinion of contemporary Old Testament scholars is that Israel's possession of this divine knowledge was due to God's definite and overt action, that this whole matter is by no means to be taken as something mainly subjective, in the facile vein of comparative religion, but rather as the record of revelatory events through which a new and powerful factor enters the stream of history from a source outside. What we are studying here is an experience of God's power, in a setting that is tremendous and awe-inspiring, surely in a very particular concreteness, yet in a manner and with a message that are decisive for all time.

This period, which is that of Moses (13th century B.C.), is the time when the really dynamic aggregation of biblical events takes place, and consequently the center of gravity for our study of the Old Testament. The earlier, preparatory phases seen in the antediluvian and patriarchal periods appear to have received their character to a considerable extent, as has already been suggested, from the memorial evaluations of a later viewpoint that was formed largely by the distinctive impetus of the Mosaic era. If this was indeed the case, the maturer events must be regarded as the basis upon which alone the early history could be completed, the motives and constructs of an adequate interpretation being available only in the light of the Exodus history. This view would recognize an inter-dependence of the two periods: the earlier upon the later for its historical completion; and the later upon the earlier for certain actual situations, such as the emergence of a national identity and the most primitive recollections of a sense of peculiar destiny and divine guidance in the experience of the Hebrew people. But the net effect of this relational concept is to place the locus of the historical dynamic in the time of the Exodus. The ideas which have been prefigured and more or less vaguely actualized in the earlier history, stand out with full force and clarity, and with a remarkable religious integration, in this decisive epoch. A people who have tended toward an historical mission and glimpsed shadowy intimations of it in memorable, solitary leaders, now find themselves consciously and unitedly committed to a peculiar world destiny.

The deliverance from Egypt made a profound theological impression upon the Israelites. So completely did it demonstrate the fact of God's guidance and protection that it was to serve forever thereafter as the type of His abiding faithfulness and truth. It was the prologue to His terrible yet gracious self-disclosure through the giving of the Law, the establishment of a most binding and everlasting Covenant, and the varied ministrations of an appointed leader who, amidst thunder and lightning, dense smoke and dire warning, had conferred with Jehovah Himself "in the mount." Under a pillar of cloud by day and of fire by night the chosen nation moved perilously onward, away from the frightful manifestations of Sinai toward the promised land of divine fulfillment. In such an existential sector of occurrence did the religion of Israel assume its definitive, providential, dynamic form.

We cannot reconstruct these Exodus events by seeing in them only a peculiarly fruitful interaction of natural and existential, actual and potential, factors. The events in themselves are nothing unless filled with the religious meaning toward which they point. At the heart of the revelatory event is mystery. The fact-in-itself eludes us, forasmuch as the wholly specific fact is a barren and unknowable terminus. Only as it comes into relation with other living and contemporary facts, and even with implicit future events which will return to lade it with still deeper meaning, does it have any actual content. It comes about, in this wise, that the happenings of Israel's desert sojourn are not just what they were "in themselves," but what they are in the light of their relational endowment, in the ultimate identity which inheres in their total, incalculable, yet plainly visible effect.

It was in this setting of extraordinary occurrence, in which the desert itself inclined powerfully toward the transcendent, that Moses had his memorable encounter with God. It was here, on "holy ground" that he heard God's call, commission, and new revelation: "I AM THAT I AM."[4] And whatever Moses may have learned from the religion of Jethro, there can be no doubt of the continuity of this new divine concept with Israel's past experience of God. For immediately (vs. 15) "God said moreover unto Moses, 'Thus shalt thou say unto the children of Israel, The Lord God of your fathers, the God of Abraham, the God of Isaac, and the God of Jacob, hath sent me unto you: this is my name forever, and this is my memorial unto all generations.' "

This title conveys the idea that the God of their fathers is absolutely faithful and may be relied upon completely in the future as in the past. Through this name He tells His people that He is really and truly present, and is ready to act and to help, as He has been heretofore.

So interpreted, it is not difficult to see how this particular revelation of the divine name provides the occasion for a great renewal of the covenant-idea. The profound and all-inclusive embodiment of this concept in the life of the nation is the outstanding characteristic and chief historical resultant of the religious dynamism of this period. Every phase of their cultic observance as well as of their teaching and their ethical conduct had its covenantal orientation. They know themselves to be a select people, bound to serve God; and their God was one who would forever protect their interests. The relationship was characterized by *hesed*, the particular covenant loyalty which was compounded of righteousness and love. It was unthinkable that the God who for His own righteousness' sake required obedience and made the most singular pledges, would ever forsake the obligation which He had assumed toward His people. As it came to be expressed in *Micah* (7:20): "Thou wilt perform the truth . . . which thou hast sworn."

The specific divine actions of this Exodus period, especially in reference to the Covenant, are the matrix in which the visible shaping of history has its beginning. By an unprecedented contact with transcendence, history is set in motion. After this tremendous revelation it is only a matter of time, and providence, until the Incarnation. The seed that is here planted can bear no other fruit. The miracle has already occurred. What follows is supremely logical, historically inevitable.

The processive motion and clearly perceptible configuration of history occur by virtue of the moral and spiritual tension exerted by the *righteousness* of God implicit in the whole of the unique transactions at Mount Sinai. As Berdyaev has noted, there comes into existence here a people obsessed by the idea of justice and its terrestrial fulfillment.[5]

The tragic continuation of this story is that God's people, chosen and challenged in this most incomparable manner, continually forsake His covenant, plumb the alternate torments of guilt and punishment for generations, taste the transforming bitterness of absolute moral failure, and finally in the tragic impotence of their desperation must look to God Himself for the realization in history of His own righteousness. Just as God must be true though all men should prove liars, so must God's righteousness be real though man should strain to the limit of his moral endurance and then perforce complete his effort in that total dependence upon God which is helpless faith. The Covenant, from the beginning, implies *grace* in prospect of man's inability. One party to a divine contract may fail; it is not possible that two should. Man's default is God's necessity—after the Covenant. So the cross itself is the climax to the historical sequence to which the revelation in the Arabian desert gives birth.

At every point along this central highway of the world's life is the spiritual tension of which real history is made; and what becomes increasingly apparent in the enlarging crisis is that God, through further divine acts of His own, must manifest His peculiar righteousness if it is ever to be seen in the land of the living. It is against this background that the portrait of the Messiah emerges as inevitably, in the logic of sacred history, as effect follows cause. The noble and strenuous morality of the prophets can have no other issue than this concept and this eventuality; for it is the paradigm of Israel's need, and the world's. In its early stage this image is extremely vague, the Messiah corresponding somehow to the nation or state of Israel, as if the one in need might yet become his own helper. Later it is a great political deliverer, or ideal Davidic king. In turn, it fastens hopefully upon a chastened portion within the nation; and finally the lone spiritual Redeemer who will manifest the character, and victorious paradox, of a Suffering Servant.

Ideas of resurrection, and of miracle in the interest of divine justice, have their rise in this atmosphere of an invincible and holy dynamism. It is the stuff of all eschatology. It is the refraction in history of the eternal holiness of God, and, up to a point, it is a process as observable as any which natural science could discern, but only up to a point. When that point is reached, an impassable discontinuity is presented. The absolute which has identified itself with time at a place called Sinai and which, with perfect *naturalness*, has been content to mingle with the course of world affairs for several centuries, must now, at a place called Golgotha, for one incomprehensible moment disengage itself from the stream of history. Yet this awful discontinuity of the cross and the Resurrection is joined by the strongest ties to the actual organic whole of history and is the indispensable core of its real integrity.

This movement is not isolated from the world outside Israel, but draws into historical community with itself a Pharaoh and a Cyrus, and later a Samaritan and a Cyrenian as well. It is a Hill of Zion toward which all national histories are gathered and to which all human cultures pay their various tributes.

It is the passion for God in history that makes the hollow period between the Testaments one burning petition for the coming of the New Age. It is this "hungering and thirsting after righteousness" which paints the lurid pictures of *Enoch* and *Baruch*, transfiguring all history into apocalypse and creating a mood of desolation so low and of expectancy so high as to reach the farthest limits. The tension becomes absolute, as the new order of existence is ready to be inaugurated. It is this world which is the threshold of the New Testament.

When the time is "filled full,"[6] there are multitudes who, like the aged Simeon, are "waiting for the consolation of Israel."[7] It is to these that the Man of the New Covenant comes, and it is to these that He speaks. With an incomparable grasp of the meaning and potency of this movement whose center will be Himself, He observes, at a moment in the midst of His brief ministry: "And from the days of John the Baptist until now, the kingdom of heaven is being forced, and violent men are taking it by storm."[8] So enormous has been the influence of the preaching of the Kingdom by the crisis-inspired, wholly devout John, and so effective the prayer concert of his followers, that the prophetic demand for the Kingdom is now utterly intense. The effect of the dedicated will of Christ can be nothing short of the actual *precipitation* of the Kingdom. On the historical side, let it be surely registered, the effective means of this precipitation are the desperate importunity and pain of this burdened servant people.

In response to His disciples' request for a pattern of prayer, Jesus instructs them to bless the name of God and then implore Him, "Thy Kingdom come." The constant and unmistakable note of His preaching is, "The Kingdom of God is at hand." The *kairos* is present. The dynamic tendency is reaching its goal. There is, hence, a deep bond, a most poignant connection between the service of violent supplication (on the part of the *biastai*, zealots of God) and the emergence of the heavenly Kingdom in history.

When His "hour" is come, He who would fulfill all righteousness makes His own decision to suffer infinitely for the sake of this Kingdom, as One standing alone and bearing in His own body the final tribulation and unutterable woe of the Kingdom-purchase.

But the sense of compulsion under which Christ moves from one juncture of His earthly life to another has reference to what is in reality far more than a sense of duty or of the interests of a literal fulfillment of prophecy. It is His sense, more than mysterious to us, of the completion of sacred process. In the words of Dr. Moffatt,

> A critical investigation of the gospels confronts us with One who believed Himself to be organically united to the divine purpose, and who was believed to have died in order to realize it for the world, not merely as a personal saviour but as the divine agent in creation.[9]

Reflecting upon this history and seeing the tragic but God-directed tendency pervading all of it, the Apostle Paul wrote: "But when the fulness of the time was come, God sent forth his Son . . ."[10] The "fulness of time" (*to plērōma tou chronou*), is one of the most pregnant terms in all the Bible, wholly fraught with tension and profound dynamic implication. The word for fulness is a substantive and comes into the writings of Paul with a very considerable distinction from its prior career in Greek philosophy.[11] It is of the essence of relatedness and process. Such being the case, it is to be regretted that the Revised Standard Version of the New Testament gives it a merely adverbial function and obscures the whole direction in which the meaning of this word must be sought.

In *Romans* Paul builds a philosophy of the past, not only of the Jews but of the race, upon this idea of historic process. A "vitalist" complexion is cast upon it in several places where the biological notion of pregnancy is made to serve as the vehicle of the concept of suffering and preparation. An example is in his observation: "For we know that the whole creation groaneth and travaileth in pain together until now."[12] It is pertinent to note that there are instances in classical Greek in which the word *plērōma*, "fulness," also has the meaning of pregnancy. Thus there is produced the thought of a direct connection between these ideas of the cosmic fulness and the pain which is the prelude to birth.

In the occurrences outlined above we look upon the continuous realization of the supreme "myth" of the will of God, a total message which is co-extensive with the dynamic structure of history. Other religions have their myths of the past, often joined to no experience of actual memory; only Christianity has its powerful myth of the future. And it is of the texture of the real. The rise of the messianic vision, with its promise of the Kingdom, is not in primitive and erratic human fancy, but in facts of divine origin, in that sphere which is the theatre of God's action, world history.

In the structure of the biblical center of history one can see, looming and unmistakable, the pattern of a most singular sequence of events. To perceive it at all—this shape of history—is to see its clear centrality in the broad plain of man's general knowledge, and consequently to lay hold upon it as the reality of world meaning. To sense this structure, with an awareness of its true position and relations, is to experience for oneself the *intuition of total form*.

COMMUNITY OF EXTRA-EMPIRICAL AND NATURAL FACTORS

The philosophy of organism recognizes that the events of the world are not made up entirely of elements that are simply "natural" and so open to scientific investigation, but are, rather, penetrated by trans-rational factors. This means that the world exhibits cleavages and incongruities as well as cognizable relationships, and that, to put it in the words of Whitehead, "In some direction or other we must devote ourselves beyond what would be warranted by the analysis of pure reason."[13] There is a place, in other words, for the exercise of faith.

The Christian interpretation of history takes into account "supernatural" events which, in comparison with ordinary types of historical experience, are radical mutations. The revelation of God's nature and purpose in the time of Moses, the Incarnation and Resurrection of Christ, and the advent of the Holy Spirit at Pentecost are prime instances of such real mutations in history. But the whole course of events, a system which gathers up into itself the minor occasions as well as the great epochs of history, is itself a form of transcendence, an entity beyond human understanding in respect of its *ground*, yet fully appropriable in respect of its meaningful *structure*.

In this system, whether viewed from the standpoint of the Bible or that of the most advanced physical science, the transcendent is taken to mean that which exists in its own right beyond our categories of analysis and explanation, but which is not necessarily outside the range of our experience in all its modes. Even our common experience, interpenetrated with transcendent reality, is what it is by virtue of its foundation in God, the principle of all concretion and order.

THE EMERGENCE OF NOVELTY

The greatest and most manifest *novelty* in the record of man's moral and social experience is Christ. The first public reaction of His Palestinian hearers: "Never spoke man like this man," was but a faint emblem of the real, cosmic differentiation which exists between Him and the best of men and the most effective and illustrious of historical causes. Forasmuch as His central position is the place where a new and controlling dimension is given to history, and because this prerogative is Christ's very *personal* and responsible possession, He is the one Man whom a true modern can equate with the meaning and worth of human life. The relative bents of human culture attain the perpendicular only at this point. All other angles have but degrees of elevation approaching this, and are, therefore, involved in the obliqueness of historical existence. This is the true right angle and our meaningful point of contact with the transcendent reality which is God.

THE ENDURINGNESS OF THE CHRISTIAN EVENT

The historical persistence of the fact of Christ is evident in many different types of effects. One could not begin to list the monuments and institutions, the doctrines and rituals, the sentiments and services, which bear witness to this ongoing fact.

The first and most clearly unique and pertinent effect is the contemporaneousness of Christ Himself as a Person. As we will undertake to show in the further course of this study, the Christian community from the beginning presents the character of a dynamic fellowship at whose center is a living and present Lord. It is He who creates the unique community at each moment of its existence. Men's experience of the living Christ after the crucifixion is altogether in the continuity of the One with whom the disciples broke bread in the upper room. He is the continuing fact of history, not a prisoner of the dead past, not one who belongs to the fixed and finished world of the already-become. He is One who still partakes of the living, mysterious, elastic fulness of current happening.

Christ lives on, undiminished. And even in this twentieth century with its cynical bondage to materialism and its epidemic hopelessness, there are countless millions who perpetuate the experience of His first disciples, and who "know Him and the power of His resurrection." The fellowship of a memory could not produce this life; it is the incontrovertible sign of the continuing Christ.

The second fact which speaks eloquently of the enduringness of Christ is the existence of His Church. The Church cannot be fully accounted for on the basis of any other supposition than that of the continuation of the life of Christ. In a most intrinsic and historical sense it is His Body, since its life depends at every moment upon His Headship and presence. It is the one society of human beings which retains its form and character despite all the corrosive influences of a kaleidoscopic world. Only a Church that is truly indwelt by its living Lord can remain the Church *contra mundum*. The basic identity of spirit which yet prevails between the Church of today and the Church of the New Testament is a proof of the enduring Christ.

Thirdly, the whole world bears His impress. Wherever He is present He compels response. Either with or without their consent, all who have heard of Him have been altered by Him. He has given a new dimension to man's spiritual consciousness, in bestowing upon it a specificially Christian structure. This He has done by requiring every man to live and die in the necessity of personal decision. Whenever the Gospel is proclaimed it brings a crisis, so that in truth the Church, as the bearer of the Gospel, is constantly judging the world. "Do ye not know that the saints shall judge the world?"[14] History thus becomes the realm of possibility and freedom. Even sin, willful antagonism to God, assumes a Christian aspect in being what it is *sub specie Christi*. The most negative and schismatic soul under heaven cannot escape the image of this new creation. A Nietzsche is inconceivable apart from the Crucified.

So the world is ever divided by this continuing Christ into two opposite camps, the confessors of His name, and the resisters of the cross. Upon the whole world lies the shadow of this cross, and this shadow is the witness of the Christ. His Incarnation is the enduring event and He is Himself the "defining characteristic" of the one imperishable society.

THE SINGULARLY COHERENT PERSPECTIVE
OF THE CHRISTIAN EVENT

The idea of a complete fact implies immediately that such a fact will afford a unique and altogether incomparable perspective in relation to all other historical items and situations. And this principle for the determination of the primary fact is abundantly supported by the data of biblical-Christian history. The "important relation," to use an expression of Whitehead, is discovered to be that which is borne to the Christian center of history; and an infinitely wide range of facts can be co-ordinated from this point as from no other.

The ever present token of the biblical origin and formation of history, as well as of the location of its unique perspective, is the division of history into the periods before and after Christ. This circumstance is the sign neither of cultural accident nor of missionary motive. The structure of world history actually corresponds to the idea which is made so explicit in the calendar. In the abyss of time this central Christ affords a standpoint for ever so wide a reckoning of the ages of the world. This is a sober and yet an amazing witness, in our everyday experience, of the source of the world's coherence. The Christian center determines the beginning and the end of history; by this center history is constituted and from this perspective the meaning of history appears. The assertion that He is the Alpha and the Omega is far more than mystic adulation—it is the recognition of the authentic nature of universal history. True historical occurrence is not an entangled web of unaffiliated facts and indifferent tendencies. It proceeds to and from Christ. It is the stage of a divinely directed and deeply meaningful drama.

THE UNLIMITED RELEVANCE OF THE FACT OF CHRIST

How many are the decisive relations which the fact of Christ sustains to its world environment! Some are very tangible, some are purely ideal; but all are important when seen in this paramount relation.

Stanley R. Hopper is but amplifying a statement made

long ago by Justin Martyr when he writes concerning the cross, "The lines of all relations intersect it; and all the lines, no matter how extended, cannot avoid the meeting place."[15] How many contradictions meet and are resolved in this single event! Past and future are embraced here, as are time and eternity, God and man, sin and righteousness, concrete and universal, shame and glory, impotence and sovereign divine power. Concerning this latter, we may observe that Christianity alone has transformed death into salvation. Through the utmost development of power absolute disaster becomes deliverance.

The Christian event has, in the phraseology of Whitehead, a "concern" for all conceivable occasions. The most evident respect in which its unlimited relevance is found to hold true is in the sphere of human interests. It is through these human and spiritual links of the world with Christ that the physical and supposedly casual events of nature are seen to gravitate toward Him. To an impressive extent human wills have control over the elements of nature, and to a still larger extent natural occurrences depend upon their relations to human life for their meaning. For as Ortega observes, human life is "the basic reality, in the sense that to it we must refer all others, since all others, effective or presumptive, must in one way or another appear within it."[16]

Not only did God originally give to man dominion over the animal creation, but also, and as unquestionably, man is now given control of the atoms which form the base of his life in the cosmos. The electron, in consequence of this marvelous new providence, finds its higher significance in the orientation of human spirits toward that one event which is the fountain of all energies. Physical reality is subordinate to man, and man, in turn, is answerable to the perfect Manhood of Jesus Christ.

The dominance of biblical and Christian ideas in the realm of general human culture is evident at many points and indicates a wide dependence upon the center in question. Every cultural idea involving any degree of worth, whether in the intellectual, the religious, moral, or political sphere, appears as the partial enunciation of some biblical truth. As such it can be readily subsumed under the Christian idea. On the other hand, the Christian idea may not be subsumed under any other, for its breadth and depth are beyond the scope of any other. This logical distinction suggests how fully comprehensive is the fact of Christ. It follows that the true direction, from whatever point, must be from the part to the whole, from the imperfect to the perfect, from the periphery of the partial meaning to the center of total significance.

This entails that the dominance of the Christian center is not to be gauged simply in the light of those areas of culture in which the response to Christian stimuli is direct and easily recognizable. It is to be seen not only, for example, in the Christian profession of a Kagawa, but also in the Christlike *ethos* of a Gandhi. For the great saint of Indian politics is no more understandable apart from the New Testament than are the completely articulate Christians.

In the same way, there is to be admitted in the ideology of early Marxism a major debt to, and a significant variation of, a segment of moral reality whose home is the Bible. Notwithstanding the fact that its moral dynamic has been alloyed with contradictory and irreligious elements, it remains true that this movement has derived its ethical impetus in no small part from the Old Testament prophets, and its type as a directional or "eschatological" world-view from the idea of history which came to birth in the messianism of the Bible as a whole. So it can be said that to a very considerable extent the Marxist philosophy reflects the structure of biblical history and corresponds, in a general way, with an early stage of biblical thought. It is fully significant only from the Christian perspective. It is an illustration of the fact that every historical reality is to be seen in relation to the Christological center. As it can be shown that every later historical phenomenon subordinates itself to sacred history, so does it also appear that in the beginning of the biblical structure and throughout its later formation this movement drew into itself, with a most superior process of selection, various cultural elements which could participate in its purpose. Thus there are Egyptian and Babylonian, Midianite and Persian motifs which are brought into the service of the central historical development. These have to do with such varied subjects as the form of the monotheistic concept, legal codes, accounts of creation and other primeval events, various messianic ideas, and cosmogonic teachings concerning "powers and principalities," angels and demons. Some of these instances we will have occasion to deal with later.

THE CENTRALITY OF THE CROSS

It should especially be noticed that the cross is the type and elucidation of all possible experiences of *crisis*. This applies invariably whether one thinks of the crisis of the individual life, the crisis of an historical epoch, as of the present, or the crisis of all time which is at the start of the Christian era. All particular crises point to the cross as to their ground and may be resolved within this supreme divine-human crisis without exhausting the potential relations of this event. The cross, at the intersection of whose staggered beams all significant relations meet, is in fact as well as in symbol the world's prime instance of historical comprehensiveness. To have a knowledge of this cross, with its unique ingathering of scattered histories, its judgment and re-creation of all cultures, its universal message and inescapable emotion, is to have a sense of the world and to be led along the path of its meaning. For as St. Paul has expressed it in language that is still philosophically adequate, "He is before all things, and by Him all things consist."[17]

The last category, which fulfills the organismic concept of *satisfaction* and to which we give the more familiar name *meaning*, has as its methodical aim the exploration of the complete event with regard to "the evaporation of indetermination" (Whitehead) or, what amounts to structural clarity and communicative orientation. This category is not one that is placed alongside those which we have already described; it rather participates in, and is characteristic of, each of the other categories. It is the concomitant of each one considered singly, and the synthesis and product of all of them when considered together. In other words, meaning appears directly in our awareness of the historical structure itself, whether it comes through one relational category or another.

In addition to this, however, there is a development of meaning which issues from the act of *interpreting* this theological structure in respect of the facts that are in closest proximity to the Personal Center of this event. The chapter on "Christ and the Being of God" will examine this interior meaning.

The present stage of our investigation may be summarized in the threefold proposition: that there is in history an actual processive structure; that this structure is distinctly recognizable; and that the act of recognition, being no less than an *intuition of total form*, amounts to a real experience of religious knowledge.

4

Christi and Historical Mission

"He was crucified as a messianic claimant and without the messianic claim the crucifixion of Christ is meaningless." —RUDOLPH OTTO [*The Kingdom Of God And The Son Of Man*, pp. 228, 229]

THE history of the messianic hope and of the process which it set in motion centuries prior to the time of the New Testament is the indispensable source of an understanding of this event in its immediate, actual character. The original impulse of Israel's unique experience of a divine Covenant and the tensional development of the intervening Old Testament history are to be kept in mind as the wellspring of the maturity of messianic occurrence which we find in the New Testament. This period, however, does not exhaust the historical preparation that is now visible to scholarship. There is the immediate context of the messianic decision, which is of very special interest.

THE RISE OF THE MESSIANIC MOMENT

Between the Old and New Testaments there is an extremely important segment of messianic development which is recorded with great vividness in the Apocalyptic and

Pseudepigraphal writings of late Judaism. Indeed, their importance is such that it can be said of them, as of the Old Testament Scriptures, that they are wholly indispensable to a comprehension of the messianic process. Especially in the last hundred and fifty years before the birth of Christ, this literature reveals a striking theological continuity with the two Testaments which are its chronological boundaries. Because of this significant continuity, and especially because of a number of original concepts which emerge in this period and carry over into the thought of Jesus and His interpreters in a very illuminating manner, it is appropriate that this *inter-testamental* material be looked at carefully.

The Books of *I Enoch, Baruch, 4 Ezra, Psalms of Solomon, Testaments of the Twelve Patriarchs*, and *Fragments of a Zadokite Work* are the ones which figure most prominently. All of these reveal a high degree of ethical and religious feeling, an impressive general similarity to biblical ideas and expressions, and a distinct progression of messianic doctrine. Their relevance to the problems of Christological research is so far superior to that of the much publicized Dead Sea Scrolls that their general neglect is hard to account for. They are, of course, rather closely related to these Scrolls and give evidence of the same thought-world.

Manifestly the late apocalyptists felt that they were divinely inspired, and their writings are marked by deep religious fervor. They appear to have been true prophets of the people, and though they were vividly aware of the political convulsions which prompted much of their teaching, they were intensely concerned with the spiritual condition of individuals. In the spirit of the ancient prophets they exhorted men to live righteous lives in the certain knowledge that the Judge of all the earth, whose purpose men see in history, will do right.

R. H. Charles, who made a very extensive study of this material, champions its high moral and religious quality with enthusiasm, and vigorously opposes the idea that prophecy and apocalyptic are to be distinguished on the ground that prophecy is ethical while apocalyptic is only the husk which Christianity sheds when it ceases to need it. The apocalyptic ethic, he insists, is based on the essential righteousness of God, the confident theme that: "God reigns, and righteousness shall ultimately prevail." Charles even goes so far as to say, "The ethical teaching . . . in apocalyptic is a vast advance on that of the Old Testament, and forms the indispensable link which in this respect connects the Old Testament with the New Testament."[1]

To this we may add the tribute of Rudolph Otto: "The conception of the Son of Man as found in late Judaism belongs . . . to the most lofty conceptions that have ever appeared in the realm of religion."[2]

The "pseudepigraphal" works are so called because their writers took the names of famous characters of the far-distant past, not only in order that their messages might have more weight with their public, but more especially that they might escape the disapproval of the current religious authorities. In an age of legalism no encouragement was given to those who aspired to fresh prophetic vision for their literary pronouncements. The day of inspiration was officially past. Thus these *inter-testamental* books are really the "underground" phase of the prophetic movement. This circumstance partially accounts for the fact that these once profoundly influential works have not usually received the recognition which their actual place in biblical history merits.

The most important of these writings is *First* (or Ethiopic) *Enoch*. Its several portions are believed to date from 170 to 64 B.C. It is partly in Aramaic and partly in Hebrew, and shows strong Babylonian and Persian influences. It appears to have been held in high esteem by the early Christians, a brief but definite quotation from it appearing in the New Testament *Epistle of Jude* (verse 14, in which there is an allusion to Enoch as "the seventh from Adam"). It was recognized as Scripture not only by this New Testament writer but also by Church Fathers in the third century, including Clement of Alexandria, Irenaeus, and Tertullian. Its influence is very apparent in numerous passages in the New Testament and there can be little doubt that its teachings did much to form the ethical and messianic ideas of Jesus.

Its doctrines concerning the "*Son of Man*," the nature of the messianic kingdom, the resurrection (and Sheol), angels, demons, beatitudes and exhortations reveal a definite kinship with the New Testament ideas on these same themes. Enoch's notion of Elijah as the forerunner of the Messiah, and his teaching of the hiddenness of the Messiah (corresponding to the messianic secret of the Gospel of Mark) are two important features which are not found in the canonical Old Testament and which Enoch has evidently contributed to the New Testament doctrine of the Messiah.

Charles, in his monumental edition of the Apocryphal writings, has shown that there are scores of expressions in the New Testament which are clearly dependent upon the phraseology of *Enoch*. Many are exact reproductions, while others are so similar as to leave no doubt that a familiarity with this work moulded many of the expressions that are found in the Gospels and the Epistles. Some of these which are either verbatim or closely approximate are the following phrases of New Testament eschatology: I John, "walk in the light," "the darkness is past," "Love not the world nor the things that are in the world"; Pauline epistles, "Angels . . . principalities . . . powers," the "light in the face" (of Jesus, or of the "holy, elect" of *Enoch*), "children of light," "in whom are hid all the treasures of wisdom and knowledge," the pain of a woman in travail (variously worded), "the angels of His power", "worthy of all acceptation," "King of kings and Lord of lords"; The Acts of the Apostles, "none other name . . . whereby we must be saved," "prayers" as "a

memorial before God"; The Gospels—John, "He hath committed all judgment unto the Son"; Luke, "your redemption
draweth nigh"; Matthew, "When the Son of Man shall sit on
the throne of His glory," "inherit eternal life," "prepared for
the devil and his angels," ("prepared for the hosts of Azazel,"
in *Enoch*), "It had been good for that man if he had not been
born"; The Revelation of St. John, imagery of the Lamb, and
of the "sea (earth in *Enoch*) giving up its dead," "The tree
of life," "clothed in white raiment," "round about the throne
were four living creatures" ("four presences" in *Enoch*, but
still about "the throne"), "the prayer of the righteous for
judgment," "angels of the winds," "a star from heaven fallen
to the earth," "cast into the lake of fire" ("cast into the fiery
abyss").

Charles' careful study has shown that four titles afterward
reproduced in the New Testament are applied to the *personal*
Messiah for the first time in literature in the Parables of
Enoch. These are "Christ," or "the Anointed One," "the
Righteous One," "the Elect One," and "the Son of Man."[3]
These titles make more definite the comparatively nebulous,
though supremely spiritual, messianic concepts that arise in
Deutero-Isaiah. They give currency in Israel to the lofty
truths contained in the Suffering Servant, and in other messianic ideals of the Old Testament as well. In *Enoch* the portrait of the ideal Messiah King emerges very clearly. And
though He is a thoroughly "celestial" figure, He embraces a
surprising number of the characteristics which are normally
associated with Christ.

A connection appears between the Apocalyptic Christology and that of Deutero-Isaiah in the fact that in *Baruch* and
in *4 Ezra* the Messiah is designated by God as His *Servant*.

The relation to *Daniel* is apparent in the eschatological use
which is made there and in *Enoch* (in highly developed form)
of the term, "Son of Man." With reference to this, Goguel
remarks that "The author of the Book of Enoch always says,

'This Son of Man.' Thus he is alluding to an earlier conception which was already familiar to his readers. He interprets the impersonal Messiah of the Book of Daniel in a personal sense, and thus he constitutes an intermediate link between Daniel and the Gospels."[4] It appears that the common source from which both writers have drawn is the Iranian apocalyptic. There is presented, accordingly, the larger and very significant synthesis of the Eastern "Son of Man" concept and the doctrine of the Jewish Messiah, a synthesis in which a transcendent celestial being is joined to the essentially moral and political messianic concept of ancient Israel. This ideal fusion of two such separate concepts helps to account for the eschatological tension in the actual career of Jesus; for, as we shall see at a point farther on, the historic Messiah appropriated this existing synthesis and immeasurably enriched it with what was the first full appreciation of the part of the Suffering Servant. Only in the mind of the historic Christ, and in the deed which His mind and heart effected, was there a perfect combination of the three: the Apocalyptic Son of Man, the ideal Davidic King, and the Servant who was wounded for many transgressions.

A very noticeable stage of the inter-testamental development is exhibited in the *Psalms of Solomon* (First Century B.C.) The passage 17:21-46 sets forth a composite portrait of the son of David, as the king of the golden age whose features are derived from many portions of the Old Testament, who is extraordinarily righteous, instructed of God, and "the Lord's anointed"—which is literally, "the Christ."

Enoch 48:2-10 makes it abundantly clear that "the Lord's anointed," before whom kings and potentates of the earth fall never to rise again, because of their denial of Him, is the same as the "Son of Man." He is the Righteous One, the Chosen One, the "Christ," who since before the creation has been with God in heaven!

A comparison of two similar apocalyptic passages, the one

from *Enoch* and the other from *The Gospel of Matthew*, will illustrate why many students of this subject consider that Jesus was greatly influenced in His thoughts and expressions by this vivid and profoundly moving doctrine.

In chapter 62, *Enoch* describes the vision which has been vouchsafed to him, of the Son of Man in the exercise of judgment. This One whom the Lord of Spirits has chosen and "with whom dwelleth righteousness" is now with the Ancient of Days, whose head is white like wool. The account follows:

> The Lord of Spirits seated the Elect One on the throne of his glory and the spirit of righteousness was poured out before him. . . . And there will stand up in that day all the kings and the mighty and the exalted and those who hold the earth, and they will see and recognize him how he sits on the throne of his glory, and righteousness is judged before him and no lying word is spoken before him, . . . and one portion of them will look on the other and they will be terrified and their countenance will fall and pain will seize them when they see that Son of Man sitting on the throne of his glory, . . . and all the elect will stand before him on that day. And all the kings and the mighty . . . will supplicate for mercy at his hand. Nevertheless . . . the angels of punishment will take them in charge to execute vengeance upon them, because they have oppressed his children and his elect. And they will be a spectacle for the righteous and for his elect. And the righteous and elect will be saved on that day . . . and the Lord of Spirits will abide over them, and with that Son of Man will they eat and lie down and rise up for ever and ever.

The parallel passage in *Matthew* is in chapter 25:

> When the Son of Man shall come in his glory and all the angels with him, then shall he sit on the throne of his glory, and before him shall be gathered all the nations, and he shall separate them as the shepherd separateth the sheep from the

goats, and he shall set the sheep on his right hand and the goats on his left. Then shall the King say unto them on his right hand, "Come ye blessed of my Father, inherit the kingdom prepared for you from the foundation of the world, for I was hungry and ye gave me meat, I was thirsty and ye gave me drink, I was a stranger and ye took me in, naked and ye clothed me, sick and ye visited me, in prison and ye came unto me.". . . Then shall he say also unto them on the left hand, "Depart from me, ye cursed, into everlasting fire, prepared for the devil and his angels: for I was an hungred, and ye gave me no meat: I was thirsty, and ye gave me no drink." . . . And these shall go away into everlasting punishment: but the righteous into life eternal.

That there is evidence of some literary connection here is almost beyond questioning. In both accounts we see "the Son of Man," sitting "on the throne of his glory," and in the background the idea of the past oppression of the righteous, the Lord's elect. In both passages, the righteous are rewarded, while the evil-doers are condemned to very similar punishments and torments. Since *Enoch's* expressions were formed first and were well known at the beginning of the first Christian century we can only conclude that the passage in Matthew is in some measure based upon it. The Gospel account is much the more magnificent, poetic and skillfully beautiful, and appears to be a refinement in the mind of Christ of the comparatively laboured original. But the connection remains and illustrates the messianic progression.

Because the eschatology of *Enoch* and similar inter-testamental books provide so much of the framework and mode of expression of the Gospels, and because in large measure it appears to have formed the mental climate of this period—the thought-world of the "multitudes," the disciples, and even of our Lord Himself—it comes to be of great importance to biblical studies. The bizarre, and sometimes barbarous, character of Apocalyptic, coupled with exclusion from the sacred canon, brings it about that this is a difficult and unwelcome circumstance to many Christians. If this is so, one can console oneself with the knowledge that in these not so reputable books we reach the mental and theological background of the people who lived in nearness to Jesus Christ.

Numerous situations in *Enoch* are so similar in mood and essential idea to passages in the Gospels that the agreement can be attributed only to a profound cultural determination. For example, the idea in *Enoch* 48:6, of the Son of Man's being "hidden" before the creation of the world and revealed only by God at the proper moment, connects closely with the many occasions on which Jesus cautions secrecy about His own identity, and with His saying to Peter at Caesarea Philippi that the Father in heaven, rather than flesh and blood, had revealed the messianic truth to him. Another instance is the passage (62:14, 15) in which the righteous and redeemed elect are pictured as sitting down and eating with the Son of Man. Jesus, in the Gospels, speaks of the time when He shall sit down and break bread with His disciples in the Kingdom of God. In both records, likewise, there is the idea of the earth and the nether world giving back their dead to share in the glory and blessedness of the time of the Son of Man's final victory (*Enoch* 51:1f).

Hardly less striking is the similarity of other apocryphal books to the thought-world of the New Testament. Here also a lofty spirit of righteousness is pervasive. If the constant theme of *Enoch* is, "Love uprightness, and walk therein" (91:3), an equally noble ethic of benevolence appears in the *Testaments of the XII Patriarchs*, which comes at the end of the second century B.C. In the section Gad 6:3 we find: "Love ye one another from the heart; and if a man sin against thee, speak peaceably to him, and in thy soul hold not guile; and if he repent and confess, forgive him." Another writing which bears the name of Enoch, the *Second* or "*Slavonic*" *Enoch*, has beatitudes that come much closer to those of

Jesus in style and ethical content than do any comparable materials in the Old Testament.[5]

A remarkable number of correspondences with the New Testament come to light in the brief *Fragments of a Zadokite Work*. Written toward the close of the first century B.C., probably between 18 and 8 B.C., this Hebrew document is all but contemporary with the life of Jesus. It represents a body of reformers within the priesthood who called themselves "Sons of Zadok," and who were the leaders of a party known as "the penitents of Israel." This group established a "Covenant of Repentance" and were extremely active in creating the eschatological pressure of these years just prior to the birth of Christ. It has been surmised that they were the "great company of the priests that became obedient to the faith" in *Acts* 6:7.

This movement was intensely ethical and religious, and it reveals a very strong and bitter antagonism against the Pharisees. This is one of a number of Gospel motifs appearing in the Zadokite fragments. Others are: the efforts of these more or less unofficial priests to reform irregularities connected with the temple; their missionary activities among the cities and villages of Israel; their insistence upon the worth of the prophets along with the Law; definite belief in divine predestination; and a rigorous opposition to divorce. Not only are there these doctrinal affinities with Christ's own characteristic emphases, but there are also historical details which tend to bring this document into very close touch with the history contained in the Gospels. For example, the incident of Herod's putting his two sons to death in the year 8 B.C. (chap. 12) opens directly upon the slaughter of the infants recorded in Matthew 2:16. Messianic variations of this book include its description of a "teacher of righteousness" who will come "in the end of the days" and be active for a period of forty years just prior to the coming of the Christ Himself. Through the time of evil a remnant shall be found to maintain their faithfulness (*Zadokite Work* 2:9). Students of the Dead Sea Scrolls will note affinities with this document.

The Testaments of the Twelve Patriarchs made a distinct contribution to the religious thought of the New Testament era. Written about 109-106 B.C., this composition gives evidence of having definitely influenced the New Testament Scriptures, including notably the Sermon on the Mount and the writings of Paul, as in his several "heavens" of spiritual vision, and scattered phrases, such as "for the wrath is come upon them to the uttermost" (I Thessalonians 2:16—Testament of Levi 6:11), and "Overcome evil with good" (Romans 12:21—Testament of Benjamin 4:3). Its teaching on forgiveness is conspicuously similar to Jesus' words on this subject, and it has also the "two great commandments" in somewhat different form.

The net impression which one receives from the whole range of this pseudepigraphal literature at its best is that there existed upon the eve of the Christian era not only a messianic atmosphere of powerful urgency but also a highly developed messianic theology.

The existence of such a well articulated theology at the beginning of the first century makes the actualization of the personal Messiah historically understandable in a far greater degree than it could ever be apart from this development. And it does something else—it explains in a measure how the interpretation of Christ by the New Testament writers could proceed with such rapid maturity. This is the circumstance to which Guignebert, for example, refers when he makes the very astute remark: "For, if we analyse the Pauline Christology and remove from it everything peculiar to Christianity (there remains) a kind of pre-Christian Christology."[6] The presence of this ripened Christological concept, incorporating the Old Testament strands and combining with them extra-canonical ideas of both Palestinian and Iranian origin, impinging constantly upon the entire moral, political and psychological existence of the worthiest element of the Jewish nation, and incessantly demanding fulfillment—is the primary fact for the investigation of the unique occurrence in which this poignant world-tendency reached its climax. The use to which Jesus of Nazareth put this heritage of a Christ-Idea in His purpose to transform prophetic promise and existential desire into historical actuality, is a record in comparison with which all other personal exploits seem commonplace and uninspiring. We must say "personal" rather than "human" exploits because it would be incorrect to regard this as a simply human performance. The consolidation of human and more-than-human agency is fully evident in the character of this event.

Owing to the teaching of the Apocalyptists great masses of the people cast their religious ideas thus around the coming of the Son of Man, and the near approach of the end of the world. These are the "multitudes" who appear in the Gospel accounts. They flock to the Jordan Valley to listen to the mortally earnest John as he preaches to them of "last things." They line the hillsides of Galilee to hear One who speaks with a new and arresting authority on the signs of the times.

The idea which these multitudes held of the Messiah was a popular blending of all the teachings that had reached them on this serious and vivid topic. It is a *median* concept that affects them and not the specific Messiah-doctrine of any particular writer or school. Nothing could be more futile than the attempt to show that this public religious mind would make conscientious distinctions between the various sources out of which their composite idea had come. Certainly there is no reason to think that they would have given preference to what we would regard as a "canonical" or ecclesiastically approved concept. The records do not suggest that the desperate common folk of Israel were especially orthodox in this late crisis. Indeed, if there was such a thing as a messianic orthodoxy, it was that current style which looked for miracles, forerunners, secrets, demon-manipulation, cloud-riding, and various and sundry celestial categories which had almost altogether arisen since the time when the lids were closed on the Old Testament canon. These manifestly eschatological features were the authentic marks, lurid and irrational as they may seem, of the advanced stage—the essential moral condition—of the world process as it is when it has reached the farthest limit of the historical negation of divine justice. As such they were valid, and we need not wonder that the foremost candidate for the messianic office accepted them as valid, and in His own thinking welded them with the best prophetic insights that the Old Testament had bequeathed to this same process in its earlier phases.

It is clear that the apocalyptic layer, being the more recent, was most congenial to the actual experiences of the nation in the periods of Seleucid and Roman oppression. As such it thoroughly conditioned the older, more definitely Palestinian strains. Yet no effective part of the older impulse was lost, in this late, popular synthesis. The great moral force of the Old Testament prophets has come down directly through these channels.

In the light of the extant literature, it would not be possible to overestimate the moral fervency of this widespread messianic concern. Reference has been made already to the groups of "Penitents" who arose among the people as an indefatigable *praying community* determined to force the realization of the Kingdom of God by a program of violent supplication. These came mostly from the stratum which, in the Rabbinic writings, is called *am ha-aretz* (literally "the people of the land"). They were the common people of Israel. In the eyes of the most privileged class they were "mean" and "poor." They were regarded as non-practicing Jews, and therefore faithless, by the upholders of the Law. They had been too busy making a living to learn how to say the Shema and the benedictions of the morning and evening liturgy; and they did not always tithe. Having a moral and instinctual rather than a legalistic and institutional type of religious experience, they were of the sort who appeared to Jesus to be closer to the Kingdom of Heaven than many of the Scribes and Pharisees. They were the "sinners" who were no better than publicans, yet far better, from Jesus' standpoint, than those who were content with their self-righteousness.

The brunt of oppression which these common people had borne had instilled in them a humility that the elders of Israel entirely lacked. Out of them, accordingly, came the unheralded but authentic "remnant" through whose reverent and long-seeking pain the messianic process was being completed, in these years in which the "fulness of the times" was reached. Their ardent longing for the vindication of God's faithfulness is both predicted and echoed in the words of *Enoch* (47:1, 2):

> And in those days shall have ascended the prayer of the righteous,
> And the blood of the righteous from the earth before the Lord of Spirits . . .
> That the prayer of the righteous may not be in vain before the Lord of Spirits,
> That judgment may be done unto them,
> And that they may not have to suffer for ever.

Then there follows the triumph of those who have invested their sorrows in God's righteousness: (verse 4) "And the hearts of the holy were filled with joy; because the number of the righteous had been offered. . ." This "number" of those who are penitentially offered would appear to be the background of Jesus' thought concerning the *extent* of messianic tribulation which must be undergone before the coming of the Kingdom. This thought is an essential ingredient of the larger idea of the fulness of the times. It is one of the factors which indicate a definitely *qualitative* (in the sense of process and content) meaning of this term *fulness.* Time itself is *different,* is tremendously potent and creative in the moment in which the process attains its climax.

This actual fulness which accrues from prayer and sacrificial suffering is pictured in *IV Ezra* in a way which illuminates St. Paul's metaphor of the woman in travail, as it conveys the idea of cosmic conditions being fulfilled in preparation for the hour of divine justice. Ezra (4:35 ff.), having proved his own faithfulness by being one of those who died for righteousness' sake, enquires of the Lord of Spirits, "When cometh the fruit upon the threshing-floor of our reward?" To which the archangel Jeremiel replies:

> Even when the number of those like yourself is fulfilled!
> For he has weighed the age in the balance,
> > And with measure has measured the times,
> > And by number has numbered the seasons:
> Neither will he move nor stir things,
> > Till the measure appointed be fulfilled.

Ezra then tells the reader of the assignment which the Lord of Spirits in turn addressed to him, as if to verify the natural certainty of this ultimate fulfillment: "So he answered me and said: Go and ask the woman who is pregnant, when she has completed her nine months, if her womb can keep the birth any longer within her? Then said I: No, Lord, it cannot."

So ineluctable is the coming of the crisis-filled hour of the new divine order.

These images of apocalypse suggest what must have been the widespread feeling of this time of incomparable tension. It is evident that irrestible prayer was the major human factor in this hastening of the world-organism. It was literally a *precarious* time, inasmuch as the word signifies "full of prayer" (*precari* plus *osus*). There is a vital difference between an era that is only dangerous and one whose danger issues in absolute supplication. The twentieth century, for example, for all of the seriousness of its crisis, is not yet precarious in this original sense.

When Jesus comes upon the public scene, there is one very particular manifestation of the lateness and ripeness of the messianic process: namely, the personality and ministry of John the Baptist. He is, for the eyes that can see it, the "Elijah" who comes before the Son of Man. His dire, prophetic earnestness and the atmosphere of judgment which surrounded his discourse had led some to ask, even, whether he might not be the Christ they awaited. So impressive are the circumstances of a career which in several respects parallels that of Jesus, that some scholars believe that John may at some point have aspired to something more than the role of forerunner. Some scholars, emphasizing the differences which arose between the disciples of Jesus and John over baptism, along with some other signs of aloofness, make the frank and rather extreme assertion that the two leaders are rival Messiahs. Whether John had such an ambition or not, it is safe to conclude that the total impact of his stern, judgment-centered message and of the sheer self-abnegation of the man himself, was to accentuate mightily the sense of finality into which the time had come. He was a visible and audible symbol of the inner character of this "fulfilled" time.

Before John, the devout could only look forward to what was essentially future. John denotes the active, emergent stage when the Kingdom is imminent, "at hand," "in your midst"; though, of course, it was not John who applied these utterly appropriate expressions.

Jesus can say, "From the days of John the Baptist until now. . ." For it is he who marks the great change, and who, because he stands within the new time, is greater than any character of the Old Testament or indeed any "that is born of woman." This is the time when prophecy is superseded, the time of *occurrence,* when John's great associate will define the moment that looms so heavily at the end of an age. The ministry of John is coextensive with the last preparatory stage: From the days of John the Baptist until now, the Kingdom of God is being forced. Strenuous men are taking it by storm. (Matthew 11:12)

The important thing to be seen in this whole connection is that the messianic hour had risen for the one whose destiny was linked with it. The history that had produced this hour produced also the man who could engage it. This process, though pulsating with actuality and world-relationship, is in its deeper conception providence. It is God in history.

The unique supplicatory fellowship, the sense of an absolute moral impasse on the face of history, the momentous token of the Baptist's rugged pronouncement and preparation, and, above all, the unspoken feeling of the historical process itself joined to the fact that the character of the Messiah was already largely constituted in the form of a dynamic idea which the whole of historical experience had conceived—all these factors together, comprehended in the most spiritual and uncalculating fashion, and subordinated, no doubt, to an anterior sense of mission which no historical study can analyze, nevertheless embody the most marvelous challenge and authentic divine invitation to realize the messianic promise, to the one individual who is chosen (hence most eminently fitted) for this transcendent task. This one individual is a man whom we first see in the company of John the Baptist in the Jordan Valley, but whose interest in eschatological matters has brought Him from His home in the north—Jesus of Nazareth.

This elect Galilean was a member of those circles who lived in the expectation of the Messiah and whose thought was nurtured upon those popular writings concerning "last things," which applied to their own time the eternal truths of the ancient Law and the Prophets. These strange documents which are "Pseudepigraphal" to us were, along with the

Psalms of David, the daily devotions of Israel's multitudes in these latter days. Jesus, who felt close to the "people of the land" and to "sinners," had taken deeply into His own consciousness the earnest and sympathetic words of "Enoch," "Baruch," and "the Patriarchs." The fact that He does not enforce these pseudonyms in any references to them in His teaching ministry shows that He understood well their really nameless origin. Yet His frequent, profound dependence upon them for the pattern and method of His messianic engagement—yes, even for the determination of His own personal essence—reveals the lofty esteem in which He held these household scriptures. They, more than any other body of concepts, framed the door through which He entered into the fulness of the Messianic truth of the Old Testament. If David and Isaiah are His farther beacons, Enoch and the Psalms of Solomon are the Messianic path on which He finally sets foot.

The pattern in its main aspects was already present. The man from Nazareth uniquely grasped this pattern, knew it to be destined for himself, and in a manner overleaping temporal relativity and every human reservation, entered deliberately the momentous portals of messianic possibility.

Jesus had heard those supernally thrilling words of Enoch, YOU ARE THE SON OF MAN, addressed to Himself.[7] And so hearing, He made His own all that belonged to the Messiah to do and to be. It appears in Enoch that the powerful preacher of righteousness, judgment, and the blessed new age, who is the prophet of the eschatological Son of Man, will be transported at the end of his earthly career to God; and will be exalted then to become the One whom he has proclaimed. The last prophet is on his way to becoming the Son of Man Himself.

Why was this particular individual intended to be the Christ of God? Is is conceivable that another might have filled the place that Jesus took for His heritage and mission?

Our answer must be that His very individuality was the historical counterpart of His election. Only *this* man at *this* time could have heard and answered this supreme call. Of all men this was the one who, in His circumstances and in Himself, matched the moment. We may say quite realistically, and yet without irreverence, that He was the one contender who brought the highest qualifications to this office. He knew Himself to be the destined One, the Son of Man.

Yet, precisely because He was a *man* He was confronted with the most terrible decision. A man—particularly the best of men—does not readily consent to be God.

THE REALITY OF THE TEMPTATION OF JESUS

Jesus' inner conviction that it belonged to Him to be the Messiah is bound to have occasioned for Him the experience of the most dreadful dilemma. This is true, assuredly, if we are going to attach any reality whatever to His human nature. The position of the present interpretation is that Jesus, in the completion of His messianic character and from the standpoint of the totality of the process, was both man and God. The peculiar conditions of the unity of the two "natures" will be discussed later in this study; the fact is mentioned here in order to emphasize His humanity as the primary ground of the inferences that will be drawn concerning the nature of His temptation. If one is not prepared to acknowledge fully the implications of an actual, uninhibited humanity in Jesus, the argument may carry some degree of offense. If, on the other hand, one can think of His human nature as historical and really effective, the following interpretation will appear probable.

Jesus, though drawn in the depths of His spirit to the messianic vocation, must as a highly sensitive and reverent Jew have recoiled instantly from the thought of a man's approach to divine office. In late Judaism the fully developed Messiah concept has been approximating ever more closely to deity. Jesus knows this quite as well as the elders of Israel, who will count any man a blasphemer who dares to offer himself in the name of Christ. If He were really human, and moreover fully ethical, Jesus cannot but have felt a deep and painful reluctance to be the Son of God. Even the "joy that is set before Him" cannot in the beginning entirely efface this problem of His moral consciousness. But this *a priori* reason, as an inference from the basic fact of His being human, is not the only ground of our supposition that the core of Jesus' temptation was a divine-human tension surrounding the messianic vocation.

In St. Matthew's and St. Luke's accounts of the temptation in the wilderness, Jesus is said to have been tempted for forty days *before* the three specific inducements were brought by Satan. The implication is that the area of this earlier and more extended temptation is somehow to be distinguished from the clearly enunciated loci of the later approach of Satan. It is not indicated in the Gospels what part the evil spirit may have played in the original stages of this temptation. Nor does this circumstance conflict with the nature of the most devastating form of spiritual tribulation. For, as Kierkegaard has shown, the most anguished experience of temptation is not that in which the devil makes his direct and immoral appeal. Rather, it is near the heart of the God-relationship itself and has to do with goodness and truth more than with shame and transparent evil.

What we are saying is that Jesus was tempted to be God. Before there could be any question of His turning stones to bread or of His hurtling from the pinnacle of the temple, before Satan could offer any collaboration with reference to earthly kingdoms, manifestly before Satan moved into the center of the picture, this man who was the most reverent and discerning Israelite of His generation must face the question whether any son of David could become the Son of Man. In the crucible of spiritual opposites, a tragic contest of dual goods, Jesus was most sorely tried. He saw that the Word must become flesh, lest in the land of the living, hope should be utterly cut off, and the truth of God should have become a lie. For the sake of righteousness, therefore, he was tempted to be God. And—to our eternal advantage—He succumbed to this unique temptation.

That most penetrating of all psychologists of the spirit, Søren Kierkegaard, has light to throw upon this special type of religious conflict. Repeatedly in his works he refers to the highest and most crucial form of temptation under the term *Anfechtung*. He describes it, after Luther, as a *double* temptation which at once repels and attracts. *"Anfechtung,"* he writes, "is in the sphere of the God-relationship what temptation is in the ethical sphere . . . In temptation, it is the lower that tempts, in *Anfechtung* it is the higher; in temptation, it is the lower that allures the individual, in *Anfechtung* it is the higher that, as if jealous of the individual, tries to frighten him back."[8] *Anfechtung,* then, as the word itself reveals in German, means a fearful challenge, a temptation that *attacks!* And note especially how applicable this is to the temptation of Jesus: "The individual is indeed innocent in *Anfechtung* (as is not the case in temptation), but nevertheless the suffering involved is undoubtedly fearful . . . Temptation assails the individual in his weak moments, while *Anfechtung* is the nemesis upon the strong moment in the absolute relationship."[9] The foundation of this experience is in the fact that man knows himself to be human and consequently at an infinite distance from the being and character of God. He is immersed in creaturehood. This spiritual pattern of temptation is therefore "the expression existentially of the principle that the individual can do absolutely nothing of himself, but is as nothing before God . . ."[10] Surely Christ could have felt no less than this.

It was not simply to emulate the heroes of ancient times that Jesus endured temptation, though it was fitting that He, too, like Abraham and Job, should be tempted and should emerge victorious. Nor was it primarily because it was expected that the conquest of Satan should be among Messiah's functions. Again, it is not merely to anticipate, in formal and dramatic fashion, the real temptations of His subsequent career. It was not deliberately in any such specific mode as these that Jesus suffered in the days following His baptism. Rather it was unavoidable in the natural reaction of the total consciousness of Jesus to the Messianic inclination of His life. There must be this intensive searching of the soul as He commits Himself to this incomparable program.

This vocational phase of His temptation is in evidence, at least, in the recorded closing episode with Satan. It is as if the adversary knows that there is still uncertainty about the basic question; for he says, *"If* thou be the Son of God— prove it in these particular ways. . . ."

And although Jesus, when He leaves this encounter with Satan and receives the ministry of angels, has definitely decided the issue, He will for the remainder of His earthly ministry allude to it in ways that reconstruct this basic tension. The human Jesus never forgets the incredible cost, the holy scandal, of his messianic commitment. There will be a time, after the agony of a final choice, when He will know Himself to be absolutely one with the Father. But today and tomorrow He pays deference to God in ways that witness to the lingering tension:

> "Why callest thou me good? There is none good but one, that is, God." (Mark 10:18)
>
> "And whosoever shall speak a word against the Son of man, it shall be forgiven him; but unto him that blasphemeth against the Holy Ghost it shall not be forgiven." (Luke 12:10)
>
> "But of that day and that hour knoweth no man, no, not

the angels which are in heaven, neither the Son, but the Father." (Mark 13:32)

"How say the scribes that Christ is the son of David? . . . David therefore himself calleth him Lord; and whence is he then his son?" (Mark 12:35-37)

THE MESSIANIC PSYCHOLOGY OF JESUS

Jesus often uses the expression, "the Son of Man," and there can be no doubt that He uses it of Himself. Indeed it is significant that only He does use it, the Gospels never applying it to Him in the objective narrative of His ministry.

In Mark 8:38 He says, "Whosoever therefore shall be ashamed of me and my words in this adulterous and sinful generation; of him also shall the Son of man be ashamed, when he cometh in the glory of his Father with the holy angels." Though He speaks here of the Son of Man in the third person, the balanced form of the sentence makes it apparent that He identifies Himself with the celestial personage of whom Daniel and Enoch have spoken. A comparison with His words, "Whosoever shall confess me before men, him will I also confess before my Father which is in heaven," ratifies this construction of His meaning.

But there is also the unmistakable passage in Matthew 16:13: "When Jesus came into the coasts of Caesarea Philippi, He asked His disciples, saying, 'Who do men say that I, the Son of man, am?' " And the still more satisfying instance of Jesus before the High Priest: "Art thou the Christ, the Son of the Blessed? And Jesus said, I am: and ye shall see the Son of Man sitting on the right hand of power, and coming in the clouds of heaven." (Mark 14:61, 62) This passage is particularly valuable inasmuch as it equates the Messiah and the Son of Man.

Textual scholars inform us that the evidence for Jesus'

application of the title, Son of Man, to Himself is drawn from every one of our documentary sources.

Usually His reference is the oblique, indirect form of the third person. It is what Otto calls a "solemn circumlocution." It is paradoxical, hence perfectly agreeable to the historical tension which it expresses. Jesus will be, and in a sense is already, the Son of Man whom He proclaims. These references and the Messianic activities of His ministry are alike, as Otto says, "proleptic."[11] They anticipate the eschatological climax toward which all events are hastening. Jesus' consciousness of mission is so strong that the imminent realization of messianic identity is to Him already a fact. If one cares to regard it so, one may say with Otto that this paradoxical outlook is in keeping with "the peculiar irrationality which essentially inheres in a genuine eschatology."[12] It would be more accurate, perhaps, to speak of the "peculiar *rationality*" which may conceivably exist at a deeper level and exercise control in this unfamiliar sphere.

This paradoxical *futurity* of Jesus' identity with the Son of Man as a real present existent is held by many able contemporary scholars including Schweitzer, Héring, Otto, Goguel, Dodd, and Knox.

Sometimes the relation is described as "dogmatic" and "mystical" (Schweitzer), sometimes as "mysterious" and "post-existential" (Otto); but in every interpretation it appears as a dynamic, historically creative identity, accomplished by the eschatological purpose of Christ. The Son of Man is finally coincident with the person of the historic Christ.

When Jesus speaks of the august and heavenly Son of Man in the third person, He is acknowledging, and leading others also to recognize, the objective divine element in the historical fulfillment. It is by God's power alone, intimate though His mighty energies have now become with actual events, that the supernatural climax is to be reached. The

Messiah's visible and glorious advent will be an act of grace. In the supreme and vindicating moment the Son of Man will be, not humanly wrought, but divinely given.

We have considered in this chapter the psychological and human aspects of the messianic decision. These have turned our attention to the immediate historical context. Our concern will be a deeper understanding of those primary facts of the Gospel that are most representative of Christ's redemptive work: the incarnation, the atoning death, the resurrection, the ascension, and the continuing life of Christ in the living presence of the Holy Spirit.

CHAPTER

5

Mythological Mode and Messianic Fact

"Mankind is now in one of its rare moods of shifting its outlook."—ALFRED NORTH WHITEHEAD [*Adventure Of Ideas*, p. 125]

LATE Judaism, of the time of Christ, possessed two characteristics, the awareness of which is indispensable to a realistic theology. That is to say, the popular culture of this time was mythological and it was eschatological. The former characteristic is one which Judaism shared with the whole of the ancient world. Rationalistic views were only beginning to emerge in this era and the mythological worldview was everywhere supreme. The latter characteristic, however, the eschatological, is one which was peculiar to the people of Israel, at least insofar as its highly developed and dynamic expression is concerned.

A mythological culture is one which accounts for its institutions by popular stories of a graphic and poetic nature, in large part or wholly imaginary, though often profound in dramatic insight and in the awareness of a universal human wisdom. A prime example of such a culture is pre-Socratic Greece.

An eschatological culture on the other hand, as formed

in Israel, is one in which men feel that history is charged with divine purpose and is moving toward a great climax. It is marked by the presence in the world of the tensions that are posited here by the mighty acts of God. It has direction, as opposed to a cyclic and static view of history, and offers the true prerequisites of moral and spiritual depth. It is the true antecedent of every serious philosophy of history.

The eschatological milieu is essentially historical; in contrast the mythological culture is essentially reflective and extra-factual. The eschatological, being by far the more potent, has made use of the mythological. The mythological, on the contrary, is not able fully to incorporate the eschatological. This circumstance points to the task of separating the two when they are conjoined (though never quite wholly fused) in the process of biblical communication.

The relationship of these two very different cultural modes provides the framework for the task of historical interpretation undertaken in this chapter. And there are two distinct but related problems with which we are dealing. The first is to come to a clearer understanding of the facts in regard to "the historical Jesus." The second is to describe, briefly and in reference to the above named modes, the great Christological events which are the heart of the Gospel witness.

Perhaps no subject in twentieth century theology has loomed larger than the investigation of the historical Jesus. Dr. Schweitzer's famous work, published in 1906 and in translation given the English title "The Quest of the Historical Jesus" typifies this effort. Schweitzer's book and scores of others in the last fifty years have thrown valuable light upon this subject. But it would appear that, as in the case of the concluding paragraphs of Schweitzer's magnum opus, the results have been found to be rather uniformly disappointing. The reason for this, we venture to assert, is that the word *historical* has been inadequately defined, or indeed usually only assumed and not defined at all, by the Christian scholars who have labored in this area. Accordingly we have now to define this term anew and to distinguish it from the less than historical concept that has prevailed until now.

In the light of the new concepts of fact and meaning discussed in the previous chapter we can see that what has passed for historical was actually no more than the sum of *archaeological* data.

We will use the term *archaeological* in contradistinction to *historical,* to denote that irreducible minimum of historical reality that is usually spoken of as the "actual." It is what can be registered by the senses, and is therefore public, incontrovertible knowledge. The archaeological Jesus, accordingly, is what would have accrued to the world if a moving-picture camera with sound recording had copied perfectly every overt action of His life from its beginning to its end. This deposit, however, though basic to the fuller actuality of His Person, and participating significantly in His real existence, is far from exhausting the dynamic and meaningful issue of His personal history. The historical Jesus, greatly exceeding the public facts of his individual actions, can be grasped only in the awareness of the unprecedented relations which His life bears to the times and places surrounding Him, and to the matchless factors of historical interpretation that converge upon Him.

The historical Jesus, as it turns out, is not just the final residue of archaeological research, though this will be increasingly impressive, and will never be irrelevant to Christian knowledge. The historical Jesus is the historic Christ. History does not separate, but rather unifies the truth which these titles represent. For history belongs essentially to both aspects of this unitary truth. To see Jesus in the fullness of His authentic history is to know that He is one with the Maker of history, who causes history to be more than the aggregate of innumerable and unconscionable bare facts— that He is in truth the Christ of God.

That He grew up in Nazareth, as the familiar son of a carpenter, that He was drawn to the Jordan Valley, and associated there with John the Baptizer, that He Himself, after His baptism, because an itinerant rabbi, that He called followers to go with Him, proclaimed the Kingdom of God, spoke as never man spoke before to many who were profoundly moved by His preaching and acts of healing, that He aroused bitter opposition of the leaders, fell into the hands of Rome, was crucified between two criminals, was dead, and buried—that these things happened and that anyone could see them—these and similar obvious things are the archaeological substratum of the Gospel. But they are not the Gospel. The Gospel calls for a larger, deeper history.

The Synoptic Gospels are doubtless the best place in which to seek the archaeological Jesus, though assuredly they give us both more and less than this. Most nearly photographic is Saint Mark, yet even here the historical soon diverges from the plainly actual.

The Gospel of John distinctly represents the stage of a mature historical communication. It is historical in the precise sense that elements of responsible reflection and genuinely devoted interpretation are active in it. In this "spiritual" Gospel Jesus, deeply known and reverently remembered by His friends, is so interpreted that His living word is projected beyond the once audible words of His actual life-time; yet His newly spoken word is all-authentic, for these who are "his own" implement His mind and heart as faithfully as His own hands and His own lips could have served. The pithy sayings of Jesus in the Synoptics, without loss of theological fidelity, are now heard as the solemn and beautiful thematics of the Johannine discourses. Now understood as Christ, He speaks as Christ in the completed language of His Body, the "gathered-out ones" of the infant Church.

A third stage is the formulated, or definitely "Christological," Christ of the writings of St. Paul, and the Revelation of St. John. In the latter He speaks in large part through the Spirit, and in the hearts of those who are "in Christ." Yet again we hear His words, sonorous and unmistakable, in his address to the Seven Churches in Asia. Then the sound of words is stilled.

There is no point in this progression at which one can say that here the historical Jesus leaves off and the Christ of theological speculation takes over. The Christ of the New Testament is one historic Christ. The continuity of this dominant fact is invulnerable throughout the whole of the New Testament witness.

INVESTIGATION OF THE CENTRAL FACTS OF THE LIFE AND
WORK OF CHRIST

We turn now to the great redemptive facts which constitute the heart of the Christian message. In order to exhibit what the writer believes is the specific, historical character of these occurrences, the term that will be used to describe them is the designation *bridge-facts*. To elucidate and apply this term, it is necessary to relate our discussion here to the particular new concept of fact which is derived from contemporary science and philosophy, and which was introduced in Chapter II of this volume under the heading, "New Instruments of Interpretation."

In the light of this concept it is to be held that a fact is not a thing-in-itself, discrete, autonomous, containing its essence in some imagined core or center, and suggesting therefore that its reality and meaning could be discovered by a purely local analysis. A fact is, on the contrary, a relational thing, an aspect of processive reality. It is not a "solid" and simple thing, but an elusive and complex thing. It is an original, vital occurrence whose ground is God. Real facts, though in essence they are to be thought of as primal occurrences, are at this stage not fully possessed of that social and experiential character which enables us to think of them as facts of history.

They are sheer occurrence only as they exist at the limit of historical experience, and they are not so known to any human observer. To us they are facts or events only in their being realized as *occurrence plus meaning.* From the standpoint of our actual knowledge the ultimate fact is no more than an abstraction, a focal place "where something happens." Certainly we cannot know such a thing as a "bare fact." In its pure objectivity a fact is wholly beyond us, whatever its reality is in the world-ground of concretion which is the realm of creativity and of God. A fact becomes what it is humanly, an *event,* by virtue of its relations, and these are the possibility and texture of its meaning. The historical reality of a fact then is in its connections with human interests and appreciations. The important thing to religion is that whatever happens in these elusive centers of primal occurrence, birth places of fact, happens through the agency of God. It is only in their nearer and marginal movements that they become subject to human understanding.

The expression *bridge-facts* has been chosen because it pictures the idea that the reality of a fact is not to be found in its imagined core but in the adjacent areas where the particular relations of the fact in question are anchored. As a bridge spans an area which is "nothing" in relation to its own structure, a blank space which is unaffected, except relationally, by the bridge itself, so a fact consists of the structure that encompasses its location without positing its essence within the location. The bridge is based actually only on its marginal piers, and, supposing it is of cantilever construction, it extends itself across the void without need of intermediate support. By analogy a great and crucial fact depends upon, and is sustained by, its particular historical referents, a structure spread out on numerous pillars of contributing fact.

The great bridge-facts of the Bible, such as Incarnation,

Atonement, and Resurrection are to be understood in this world-relational sense.

It is not possible to do justice to the description of any fact, unless one is prepared to indicate the range of its relational system at which it is being considered. Mere analysis, at any rate, will approach a vanishing point where nothing significant remains. This is as true of the great events of Bible history as of any other. If the analysis proceeds as if these facts were "discrete" and self-contained, only disappointment and tragic misunderstanding can result.

The death of Christ may, with the reverence due this most sacred event, be taken as an example. What was this fact in itself? Leaving aside any description of its physical aspects, which probably could never have conferred more than the slightest distinction upon it (it appears to have differed in some few particulars from the deaths of other victims of the cross), we observe that the emotions which Christ displayed and the words which He spoke from the cross were most singular and Godlike. There is, even within the terribleness of this incident, the most wonderful and unforgettable restraint. These expressions, however, are not the innermost fact, they are not His death, but rather the living, sublime context of the actual death.

The general outward appearance of the death itself was such that Tacitus could refer to it in the most casual manner as to a mere fact. His brief allusion to it is not burdened with any theological meaning at all. But those persons who stood within a particular system of relations, the most impressive ever known to history, in the wake of Old Testament prophecy and late messianic longing, in the midst of the consternation of moral crisis, and at last in the constraining presence of a risen Lord, those persons, surely, could not but view the same occurrence with a wholly different sense of its meaning. To them it was the death of Christ, the Atonement, and it was this *in reality* as well as in their subjective experience because the relations of the cross were as far-reaching as the history both of the past and of the future, and cosmic in their total reference. The death of Christ was all that Christians have ever thought it to have been in their bold evaluation of this sacred event, but the full reality of it has been made dependent by God upon these relations. The fact of the cross cannot be detached from these surrounding facts and their interpretation. The important thing is not "how" a man died on Good Friday, but rather "Who" died! The dogmatic is no less factual than the biological.

The *event* of the Cross, therefore, is not confined to the death of Jesus, though it certainly could not have been without it. The death itself is the bare occurrence lodged in the heart of the most compelling unity of world-relations, which, from the human point of view, is meaning, doctrine, and spiritual experience. But what is meaning to us does not exhaust the reality of the event. It is only the historical part of it, and the determination of the whole is of God. Into the holy place of the primal occurrence as it is in "itself," no man is entitled to enter.

Something of this same type of interpretation should characterize our approach to the subsequent great event of Christ's Resurrection. To say this is not to suggest that we can ever understand the Resurrection any more than we can understand His atoning death. On the contrary, it is to point to the mystery which must always surround it, and in the atmosphere of which we have no alternative but to feel our limitation and to surrender the dogmatic attitude. The event of the Resurrection is incomparably more than we can ever determine or conceive in the way of a probable reconstruction of the physical and psychological circumstances which accompanied it in the aspects of its factuality. Nevertheless, such information as we do possess lends strong support to the long-held conviction of the Church that in a literal sense "it was not possible that he should be holden of"[1] death. In a

manner at once powerful and mysterious He overcame death
and returned to life. This belief is accentuated by Christ's
unique historical situation, with all that it implies as to
a tremendous focus of cosmic energy. To affirm, however,
that He literally triumphed over death, and that He actually
lived again in the presence of His followers, is not to say that
His resurrection is a physically observable and verifiable
phenomenon, or that the Scriptural accounts of it are true in
a literal sense. It is, notwithstanding, to be maintained that
the Resurrection is factually true and theologically meaningful. The nature of the distinctive mode of the Resurrection-
witness is a different matter to which we will return in a
moment. As for the Resurrection itself, it is the crowning
event of the world's most compelling sequence, a bridge-fact
which even the atoning death does not eclipse but which it
does profoundly motivate in the transcendent causality of
sacred history. Dynamically, as well as theologically, the two
great facts are inseparable.

The power and meaning of the great bridge-fact of the
Resurrection is not in the circumstance of its bare transpira-
tion. The literal emancipation of Christ's body from the
grave, supposing this really to have occurred, could hardly
stand in a more vital relation to His Resurrection in its fulness, than the corresponding relation of the cessation of His
breathing and heart-beat to the depth and richness of the fact
of His atoning death. In neither event can the larger reality
which composes the Christian fact be identified with the
problematical core of actual occurrence, or made to depend
upon any particular conception of it. The nature of this
inner core is shrouded in mystery, whether it is conceived as
physical or otherwise. In any case the fact extends, in a way
that is cognizable and affirmative, beyond the indeterminate
core.

Whether Christ's Resurrection is thought to embrace a
physical aspect or not, the event as a whole will certainly

not be inferior dynamically to the usual concept of a bodily resurrection, but rather will appear as a more extensive occurrence. What is most evident from the standpoint of historical science is that the Resurrection event is a uniquely potent and epochal event, and that some tremendous occurrence has taken place at its center. It is incalculable, and while it is as truly historic as any event, it is at the same time beyond history in its foundations.

Conclusively, the nature of this event could never have been confined to the activity of the religious imagination of Christ's disciples, to a grief-born illusion on their part, or to any conceivable combination of human factors, whether actual or literary. The texture of this event is infinitely firmer than that of even the most invincible mysticism. It is equally beyond the range of any literary creativity, whether individual or corporate. This event is not primarily in the nature of what men think, or even of what men hope, but of what God does in the sheer unexpectedness of omnipotence and divine grace. C. H. Dodd is making only a moderate claim for this event when he writes,

> The assumption that the whole great course of Christian history is a massive pyramid based upon the apex of some trivial occurrence, is surely a less probable one than that the whole event, the occurrence *plus* the meaning in it, did actually occupy a place in history at least comparable to that which the New Testament assigns to it.[2]

A fact of history is far from being a simple notion when one takes into account that it is never entirely distinguishable from the theoretical element which surrounds it in experience. If the same is true of the facts of science, as a number of contemporary writers have shown, how much truer must it be of religion, where the angle of human reflection multiplies this element immeasurably. The question whether a fact has meaning in *itself* is resolved into the question: what meaning is found within a particular radius of its relational circle, this radius being determined by the interest and participation of the observer? As one approaches the center, the fact will lose human significance, however much it may retain of cosmic originality and potency. Yet, following Whitehead, we are inclined to conceive of this center itself as being somehow influenced by the whole context which belongs to it; for we are committed in this philosophy to the position that wholes can determine parts as well as parts wholes. That is why it is reasonable to think that at the heart of the Gospel history there must be an occurrence that is as unique in respect of the character of event as the total movement leading up to it is unique in respect of world process. No analysis, however, can make this apparent. As bridge-facts, arching broadly over realms of mystery and cosmic truth unfathomed, these great Bible happenings must still appear to us. Even so, they are no less real as facts—but more impressive and challenging.

It is this insight into the actual complexity of facts which has led current writers of the Phenomenology school to insist that science is essentially "hermeneutics." The interest of science in *meaning* is becoming increasingly apparent, as we have shown, among several prominent types of mathematical, physical, and cultural philosophies. The favorable advantage of Christian thought in this scientific endeavor toward interpretation is that in the sphere of Scripture and theology there is found a central body of meaning which other systems, for the sake of their own instinct toward completion, cannot evade. For from the biblical center alone can it be said: nothing that is human is alien to me. The debt which every thinker owes to the concept of cultural and intellectual inclusiveness will require him to look carefully to this center.

Though we do well when we resist the impulse to rule out dogmatically the existence of physical components at the heart of the great Christological events, we are nevertheless bound to maintain that they are by no means essential to any one of the Gospel bridge-facts (except broadly the Incarnation), and there is not in the instance of any of them a really sufficient reason for recognizing the prevalence of such material aspects. At the same time, we must admit the presence and wide-spread functioning of extra-factual modes in the communication of these truths in the Scripture. The facts are clearly messianic, but the witness, or the transmission of these facts, is often in the mythological vein. The facts themselves are not "mythical" at all.

The mythological witness, making use of poetic and symbolic ideas, of the picture-language characteristic of the particular time and culture, is plainly in evidence in the Gospel accounts of the Incarnation. No small portion of the beauty and sublimity of this great doctrine is due to the reverent purity of these poetic constructs of the birth of the Savior.

The story of the crucifixion reveals a minimum of the extra-factual mode. To tell that Christ "suffered under Pontius Pilate" does not require the aid of mythological discourse. But in the background, by way of marginal motifs, there is, for example, the mention of the dead rising on the night of Christ's death and walking openly in the city. And there is also the symbolic reference to the moment of the rending of the temple veil. On the whole, however, the account of the death of Christ is factually and awesomely straightforward.

On the other hand, the Ascension, though embodying an indispensable Christian truth, a bridge-fact hardly less essential than the others, is told in a form that is almost wholly mythological. Beneath the brief picture-drama in the opening chapter of *Acts* there is the very significant fact that Christ at a certain point abruptly absented Himself from the personal presence of His disciples. For some time following the Resurrection He has been in their midst and somehow present even to their senses. Now He will be present in this manner no more. Of this change the Ascension is the formal indication. It is a great terminal idea. It should be observed, however, that in the judgment of the ablest contemporary scholars the Ascension and the Resurrection were identical in the earliest experience of Christian faith.

The influential work of Prof. Rudolph Bultmann has made vivid the need of finding a solution to the problem of the mythological elements in the New Testament. He shows that these materials are a serious barrier to the acceptance of the Bible's message on the part of a host of thoughtful people in our time. These thought-forms are descriptive of a cosmos totally different from that known to modern man. Because of this mental gulf, says Bultmann, the message of Scripture must be de-mythologized, so as to communicate to men who are conditioned by a scientific world-view. This process, the German theologian believes, must take the form of a radical translation in which the mythological ideas give way to the basic truth of the Gospel, which is conceived generically as man's confrontation with the eternal in the midst of the relative and finite.

In this ultimate situation, the pattern of which Bultmann derives largely from Heidegger, the individual is compelled to choose between God and this transient world. In effect then, Bultmann interprets the historic doctrine of salvation as a type of existential experience, and unfortunately lays himself open to the criticism that he sacrifices the Gospel for philosophy. Actually he makes a strong case for the centrality of Christ's redemptive work.

The view of the mythological problem held by the present writer will encourage a different solution. Instead of eliminating the mythological, and with it the whole body of messianic fact that is so thoroughly bound up with it, we should simply recognize the mythological as what it really is, namely the Bible's peculiar medium for the transmission and interpretation of theological truth. One cannot actually de-mythologize this history; one can only explicate the myth and thus secure the messianic reality it was fashioned to communicate.

Between the studied rejection of mythology by Bultmann on the one hand, and the uncritical denial of its very existence by Fundamentalists on the other hand, we must choose the third alternative of retaining the great myths of the Bible, for the purpose of understanding them in their true character and letting them serve our understanding of the enduring religious facts which they were meant to elucidate. We are not faced here with an impossible either-or. We need not choose between the Bible myth and the messianic fact. We should accept them both for what they are: one as the native form of eschatological discourse, and the other as the constant and indestructible truth of salvation.

When we look beyond the myth, and we may fortunately add, *through* the myth—what we see is not simply the stark and dreadful crisis of human existence. We can see this, now and then, without the help of any eschatology. What we behold through the strong, clear lens of the New Testament Myth is not the pale visage of a philosophical category, but the face of Jesus Christ.

The next subject is the metaphysical interpretation of the Christian event in the light of its unique interiority, as realized in the person of Jesus Christ. Our concern, in this connection, will be the development of a new and distinctive rationale for the doctrine of the deity of Christ. It will take the form of an Existential Christology as it continues to derive its bearings from actual history and from the nature of personal consciousness, as opposed to the methods of logical abstraction. It will provide a modern alternative to the traditional substantialist concept of a Christian ontology.

6

Christ and the Being of God

"... the God-Man is himself the existential."—SØREN
KIERKEGAARD [*Journal*, p. 374]

THE total process of history reveals a dialectical progression, and a world crisis in the events of the life of Christ which is cognate with the spiritual crisis of the life of the individual person. Both in the individual and in the universal instance there is the increasing contradiction which results from certain given facts of the moral consciousness, the arrival at an absolutely desperate incapacity for religious integration, and the salutary act of renunciation and faith through which the redemptive, peace-bestowing reversal is accomplished. What the Resurrection is on the historical plane, spiritual re-birth is in the dialectic that occurs in human life. Thus it comes about that the cross of Christ denotes a three-fold crisis: that of His own personal history, that of the religious individual, and the vast crisis of the world process.

This unparalleled relationship, which notwithstanding its dimensional aspect represents an organic unity, provides the approach to an interpretation of the Person of Christ in terms of an existential philosophy. It has as its objective not only to vindicate the fully historical character of Jesus' Messiahship, but also to present a new rationale for the postulation of

His deity, in the significant sense of a unique, essential identity with God.

The discussion of one of the foregoing chapters stressed the importance of *decision* in the messianic consciousness of Jesus. It is an idea which is in close connection with the authority and uniqueness of His person, which impressed all who saw and heard Jesus. It is only at the point of this idea of decision that His valid possession of both a human and a divine consciousness becomes manifest. Indeed this is true to the extent that it is in the dialectical area of decision that these two phases of His personality have their main historical contact. Under the idea of decision, accordingly, the most salient facts of His messianic career may be construed. Nor is this the most important thing that can be said concerning His decision. For in addition to being the determinant of His messianic mission in its specific features, it is, in view of its totality and of the unique range of its cosmic connections, the ground of His actual identity with God.

In reference to His accepted mission Jesus' decision involves a number of significant features which attribute to the corresponding events an historical character that is wholly unique. This is by virtue of the fact that the decision itself has embraced an absolutely incomparable opportunity. For what Jesus is doing is no less than this: He is uniting Himself personally with the totality of the messianic process. By an act of will which is also the profoundest recognition of His own personal constitution, situation, and destiny, He identifies Himself not only with that portion of messianic history which is already past, but dynamically also with the present and future of this singular process, this *élan vital*, of redemptive history. He chooses at once that which can be, in the infallible tendency of divine promise, with that which already *is*, in the prior accumulation of this process in reference to Himself.

Jesus' messianic decision involves three major consequences, or active corollaries, which are discernible in a very
formative aspect throughout His career. They exhibit an
order in which there is logical and chronological agreement.
These three principal steps are: (1) Identification and appropriation; (2) Actualization; (3) Completion and projection.

First in His own mind and later in the thought of His disciples and before all men He identifies Himself with the Messiah. This is not to say that He will conform exactly to any
particular Messiah-image. But in the generic sense, and beyond that in respect of His own principle of preference, selection, and emphasis, He will be the Messiah whom the popu-
larly instructed Jewish believer can recognize. When the
"woman at the well" in Samaria speaks of the Messiah whom
her people have expected, Jesus does not hesitate to say, "I
am He." When asked pointedly by the High Priest whether
He is the Christ or not, He instantly replies, "I am, and you
shall see . . ." Thus He identifies Himself with the Christ of
prophecy, the known Christ of the pious contemplation and
ceaseless hope of Israel. And as such, He appropriates the
generally presupposed features of this Old Testament Christ.

He takes to Himself the prerogative of kingly judgment,
He casts out evil spirits and heals the sick, He shows Himself
Lord even of the Sabbath day, He speaks cryptically in par-
ables, He orders a colt when He desires it for His triumphal
entry into Jerusalem, He gives His life as a ransom for many
—He does these and many other things in order "that the
Scripture might be fulfilled," concerning the conduct of the
Christ. This is His deliberate appropriation of messianic
characteristics. In the manner in which He effects it He con-
stantly makes it clear that these are the things that belong to
Him, and it "behooves" the Christ to do them. While it is
yet day He must do the works of the One who has sent Him.

This total vocational reference is indispensable to an

understanding of what Jesus came to mean, especially after His death and Resurrection, to His disciples. So complete was His appropriation of the messianic essentials that these entered vitally into the idea which His followers formed of Him as a Person. Because He made upon them such an integrated impression, we must see in this relationship (Jesus —Christ-idea—disciples) a part of the actual constitution of His Person. As C. H. Dodd has said, "the value Jesus had for those who followed Him is part of what He was."[1]

Jesus' *actualization* of the messianic mission represents a real advancement beyond the idea of His *appropriation* of it. The earlier step, identification and appropriation, has included His sense of personal right and of the available instruments and procedures which are historically fitting to the program of action which He has chosen. Actualization is the stage at which He carries out in practice the things which belong to the messianic office. Most typical of His attitude in this regard, and descriptive of His entire program, is the incident in Luke 4, in which He announces Himself in the Synagogue at Nazareth as the fulfillment of Isaiah's passage: "The Spirit of the Lord is upon me, because he hath anointed me to preach the gospel to the poor; he hath sent me to heal the brokenhearted, to preach deliverance to the captives, and recovering of sight to the blind, to set at liberty them that are bruised, to preach the acceptable year of the Lord."

As He puts into effect this signal program of divine justice and mercy, and above all as through His faith-producing witness and suffering He brings to fruition the process which God has long since inaugurated for the healing of the nations, He is accomplishing God's own purpose. Both in spirit and in historical effect He is carrying out the central and crucial action of God in history. This fact is so apparent that even the most dispassionate view of biblical history must, at the least, conclude that Jesus' messianic deeds are virtually the activities of God Himself. Other religious leaders have done God's work, but in a partial sphere of far less than universal significance. Only the historic Christ has done that total and decisive work which reason compels us to equate with the action of God Himself. Only He could assume the role and actualize it.

The originality of Jesus does not consist, as the older Liberals would have it, in His specific teachings or in some ideal aspect of His spiritual attitude. He was not the first to teach the Fatherhood of God, the beauty of forgiveness, or the blessedness of self-sacrifice. His true originality is in the manner in which He turns all ideals into historical actuality and gives to them new depths of meaning by His unique execution, as of His own purpose and task, of God's definitive work in the world. He provides a frame of reference by which all values are given a new status which isolated ideals, lacking incarnation, could never possess.

The third stage, that of *completion and projection*, carries the historical divine action of Jesus still farther. This tends to be two phases, which may be considered separately. *Completion* is that aspect of Jesus' thought and action in which He invests in the idea of the Messiah a richer spiritual content, and moreover a wholly original and creative *unity*, such as it has not known before. He has fused within Himself the various, even apparently contradictory, strands of messianic doctrine which were extant in His time. Upon this more or less incongruous and ambiguous accumulation of messianic traditions He brings to bear the clarifying domination of His own superior insight. What issues is more than a synthesis. It is a vital new concept which from its birth has the power of its own actualization. We may hazard the thought that the operation of Jesus' mind in this regard has something in common with a process known to modern psychology. That it is not more than this we would not argue for one instant; but one cannot escape the impression that in His unique intuition of the messianic idea Jesus is "closing the gap" in the manner of the *Gestalt* theory of perception. In His own thought He concludes the tendency toward completion which this organic idea possesses. In this unique intuition the fragmentary elements of messianic tradition now come to the "closure" which alone can give them full historical effectiveness. This is the heightened instance of what Cassirer has discovered in the general tendency of cultural symbols to round themselves out and to realize a kind of perfection as they mature.

In accord with this principle we find in the Gospels many instances in which Jesus has made profound personal contributions to the idea (and now reality) of the messiahship. His intimate and sustained communion with the Father is a case in point, as is also the "educational" function in which He appears in relation to His disciples as He makes them responsible for the continuation of His own messianic ministry.

The disciples, probably without clearly realizing it, were actually completing the messianic fact and impress which Jesus had begun in His own life. This is the initial phase of that which from the standpoint of Jesus is the *projection* of His messianic activity. The whole of the New Testament's interpretation of Christ is to be understood in this light. As the apostles in their teaching relate Him to the Old Testament and indicate the breadth of the fulfillment of prophecy which they can now see in His life, death, and resurrection, they are themselves engaged in a work of completion. As the Spirit of Christ speaks through them in their Gospel witness, so that a fuller experience of His personality becomes available through their devoted memory of Him, they are His own individual projection. As those who are in communion with Him make vital inferences from the facts which He has bequeathed to them, they are continuing the inexhaustible impulse of His own career.

There is another important sense in which Jesus projects His messianic calling. It is in the fact that it points finally toward a second historical climax in which all opposition to

the divine sovereignty will be overcome in the perfect realization of His Kingdom. This subject, implicit though it is in
the thought with which we are now occupied, is essentially
an occasion for religious faith and does not present data that
are useful either for historical or for metaphysical interpretation. The fact that this idea is often forced into the service of
a fanatical type of theological speculation accounts for a
considerable amount of friction that arises to do damage in
certain sectors of the Christian community today. Suffice it
to say that it has only the most specious connection with the
eschatological emotions of biblical history. The tension of
New Testament eschatology is essentially moral. On the other
hand, our current "dispensationalism" has relinquished a
real moral concern with history, and occupies itself with entirely amoral vagaries.

FOUNDATIONS OF AN EXISTENTIAL CHRISTOLOGY

To say that the historic Christ does God's work, even in
the central, redemptive sequence in which the messianic process inheres, is not quite tantamount to saying that this
Christ is God. To secure reasonable evidence of His true
deity, it is necessary to go beyond this extremely impressive
fact; although, as was shown in an earlier section of this
study, the recognition of the Christian configuration of history is indispensably valuable in that it indicates the source
of historical meaning, manifests the reality of a righteous and
sovereign God, and presents strong implications as to the
unique character of the central personal agent in this process,
whom we have shown to be both "Jesus" and "Christ." It is
true that the idea of "Christ" implies deity, and that the historical evidence of Jesus' right to this title is overwhelming.
Yet to show that this Christ is extraordinarily unique and
Godlike is still to fall short of establishing His *essential oneness* with the God who stands behind the historic process.

In the effort to give cogency to the idea of Christ's deity we can have no recourse to the older rationalism with its basis of substantialist categories. Modern thought has demonstrated the unreality of this method.

Fortunately there are within the purview of the *philosophy of existence* facts which lend themselves to a radically different rationale of Christological interpretation. With the aid of these it is possible to present a statement of the deity of Christ that has the advantage of being grounded in the concreteness of history while possessing a character that is thoroughly reasonable in respect of its specific logic as well as in the light of the broadest ideational context. It is conclusive, and it satisfies the conditions of universality which any metaphysical account is expected to meet.

The thesis that Jesus actually identifies Himself with the messianic process raises a question which will serve to introduce this formulation of an existential Christology. The question is this: Is it possible for any person to unite himself essentially with something which is not himself? Can a person really identify himself with that which is exterior to the irreducible specific entity which he himself is?

Now to this question the logic of substantialism answers that it is impossible. It must give this answer because of its concept of what constitutes the personal ego. This traditional philosophy follows the reasoning of Descartes who held that "substance" is "a thing which exists in such a way as to stand in need of nothing beyond itself in order to its existence."[2] On the basis of this definition he described "mind" as one of the two all-inclusive types of substance and repeated the affirmation that minds, like bodies, stand in need of nothing beyond themselves individually. Substantialism, accordingly, believes that the ego is a "thing-in-itself," an absolute, essentially unmodifiable, existence. This self is not thought of as being conditioned (in its *continuing* existence as contrasted with its creation) even by God! It is an autonomous object and in this respect it does not differ, in the Cartesian view, from any stick or stone. Every substantial object is essentially discrete, isolated from every other. As was earlier indicated, the roots of this objectivism are in the days of primitive science when ideas of reality were formed from visual experience unaided by any techniques or theories of analysis. When men saw an object it appeared to be solid, homogeneous, changeless. So it was assumed that the unseen reality of the self was like the substantial nature of the body. It was essentially a "thing." Descartes' definition is in an identical vein. Though he stipulates that mental substance lacks the quality of "extension," the other characteristics of a material existence remain implicit in his "thinking" substance.

Turning from this now untenable and humanly unwelcome category, modern thought has investigated and approved newer concepts which are immeasurably more congenial to the facts of personal experience and historical reality. It has to a large extent realized already the program suggested by Ortega's conviction: "In order to speak, then, of man's being we must first elaborate a non-Eleatic concept of being, as others have elaborated a non-Euclidean geometry."[3]

Whereas the ancient psychology (and consequently Christology also) approached its subject from the angle of an abstract conception of "nature," the modern view of personal existence begins with an analysis of the structure of the personality itself. And in the case of Christology we must combine with this analysis of the self a constant reference to history as the field in which the only real explication of the being of Christ can take place. It is through history alone that the doctrine of the Person of Christ can achieve its ultimate, cosmological meaning.

Modern investigation reveals that the ego is a *functional* rather than a substantial type of reality. And it must be emphasized forcibly, in opposition to mental habits of long standing, the functional and structural aspects of reality are not less valid and dependable than the supposed solidities and immutabilities of the older metaphysics.

The idea of function by no means reduces us to an evanescent and inoperable concept of the ego, such as would take from it its individual and authentic existence. As one contemporary spokesman of this point of view describes it: "The self is not an experience within the experiences, nor can it be equivalent to the whole of the experiential flux, but is 'something else'—a plus—which connects, leads and gives sense to it . . . The self is not changeless but it is permanent. It is always present and what it experiences both modifies and gives stability to it."[4]

The ego, though it has a decisive relation to it, is not the whole personality. Naïve philosophy equates the self with the total impression that is made by an individual person and proceeds to recognize in this total idea a peculiar quality as of the static *being* of this person. The view is erroneous in that it fails to take into account that this total complex of personality is within itself constantly changing and that its margins of contact with its environment are not absolutely defined but reciprocal, vague, and shifting.

There is within "you" an irreducible and constant ego, but you are far more than this ego. You are the accumulating interaction of this private core of possibility with your entire experience. You are your physical self and the sensations which this mode occasions. But you are more than your body: you are the clothing which either you or your economic situation has chosen for you to wear, and which, being next to your flesh and exposed to "others," influences you profoundly. Beyond these physically immediate relations you are (quite as really, though less tangibly) other factors which constitute your vital environment—your home, work, friends, distastes, avocations and other contacts in which you see yourself and are seen by others. You are your "self" plus your circumstances.

The assumption that real personalities are as spatially limited (and therefore as epistemologically definite) as their physical bodies springs from the fact that the biological aspect of the self is that which is most readily perceived. Because the body appears constant, and is evidently "objective," the perception of it gives rise to the fallacy that "you" are a changeless entity, quite self-contained in your substantial body-and-soul.

The new understanding of personality as constantly transcending the body has the most direct and significant implications for an interpretation of the life of Christ. It illuminates the fact that no sharp lines are drawn, in the New Testament accounts, between those activities in which He is physically present and the even more effective actions and impressions which issue from His Personality in its transcendent aspect. It makes entirely credible the peculiarly dynamic relations which exist between Jesus and those who constitute His "Body," the Church. Because of the unique dominance of His Personality, the fellowship of those who have centered their lives in Him is an actual portion of Himself. Between the fontal events at the nucleus of His own existence and the community which becomes involved in His mission there are the most potent and unprecedented relations.

The ego which dwells at the center of the personal complex is not the colorful and fully differentiated gathering of characteristics that we know in our individual acquaintances and friends. In its specific existence it is primarily a localized and continuing form of *possibility*. Its essential function is that of *decision*, and this function is so conditioned by the immediate source of its possibility that it is always characterized by a feeling of moral obligation. The experience of *anxiety* is the immediate psychological result of this possibility, but anxiety is not the essence of the primal structure itself. It is in the contact of the original structure with the "world" that the tension of anxiety emerges.

The primordial ego may be defined, then, as *a permanent center of responsible freedom*. It is formal, and its individuality consists mainly in the fact that it is *one* in relation to its source. It is personally neutral and undistinguished except for one thing: it receives its moral sense from the creative source of its constitution as an individual ego. What is ordinarily thought of as individuality or "personality" is the product of this moral ego in relation to the historical situation in which it is placed.

This permanent individualization of pure freedom is maintained directly by God. The "nature" of the ego is simply that it depends at every moment for its actual continuation upon God as Creator. To paraphrase Heidegger's penetrating expression "Being-in-the-world," we may say that the innermost existence of the personal ego is a "Being-next-to-God." The ultimate content of the theological idea of man's bearing the *image of God* is in this foundational fact of the psychic structure.

This description of the ego finds significant corroboration in Jaspers' concept of *transcendence*. This philosopher writes, "Only through freedom do I know transcendence. Through freedom I do unquestionably reach a point at which I am independent of the world, but it is through the consciousness of the radical connection with transcendence. For I do not exist through myself."[5] So Jaspers reasons that a person is "given to himself" through transcendence. It is only in this totally uncontingent relation that there is an essential equality of all men.

Man's being is in God. It is not, as substantialism would have it, that he requires nothing outside Himself in order to exist.

Such being the situation of the ego, we may observe that it is especially bounded on two sides by God: in the area in which it is constantly originated in freedom; and in the experience of actual events beneath which God is the universal ground of concretion. In an ever present creation and in an all-inclusive providence man's life touches God.

Personality is not a *thing*, but a *continuing in relation*. It is not static, but dynamic. It is not spatial, but dimensionally free. It is not a fixed object but an immeasurable potential. It is not a thing-in-itself, but a being in God.

EXISTENTIAL ANALYSIS OF THE MESSIANIC DECISION OF JESUS

The definitive contribution of the *philosophy of existence* to theology is at the point of an interpretation of the particular essence of the Personality of Christ. The locale of this investigation and of the application of its original method to the facts embracing the "Incarnation" is the *decision* by which Jesus identifies Himself with the whole of the messianic process. We propose to show that this uniquely cosmic decision is the ground of the most basic and far-reaching metaphysical construct that it is possible to formulate in reference to actual, historical data, and that it amounts to a rational demonstration of the essential identity of the Christ of history with the God of eternity.

Specifically, it is the thesis that Christ, through this total decision, establishes Himself in deity. This is the area which has been indicated in earlier references of this study to the significant *interiority* of the center of the Christian structure. It is the vertical axis of the whole sequence of occurrences which, in the language of theology, are "revelation."

The existential concept of personal being is that it is the product of choice. This postulate neither opposes nor minimizes the reality of the individual possibility (primal ego) and agency which are prior to the fact of decision. But it does maintain that the *essence* of one's personality, one's characteristic being, is consequent upon actual decision and not prior to it. It holds that being is product and not origination. This is the meaning of the maxim: "Existence precedes essence." In the most real sense *we are what we become* through choice. This totally serious decision is no less than a metaphysical option.

Existence is the act by which one passes from possibility to historical reality, from the "I will" and the "I must" to the "I am." The conditions of this act, or choice, are determined by the entirety of one's former choices and experiences. These are one's "history," and this, along with the freedom to choose, constitutes one's possibility. This historical accruement indicates the kind of person that one can be, or, more accurately, it prefigures "who" one can be. As one chooses the person who he can be, and now determines to be, he chooses his own essence.

There is in this process of establishing one's essence and authentic vocation a most vital and indispensable link with the past. Kierkegaard describes it in this way:

> So the individual chooses himself as a concretion determined in manifold ways, and he chooses himself therefore in accord with his continuity. This concretion is the reality of the individual, but as he chooses it in accord with his freedom one can also say that it is his possibility, or (to avoid an expression so aesthetical) that it is his task. . . . The individual therefore sees this actual concretion of his as his task, his goal, his aim.[6]

Since my choice is in this respect determined by the *datum that I am*, I am in a sense given to myself. But it is no static conception of being that this dialectical progression denotes. My choice is not a mere re-installation of the past. It is movement, becoming and change. It is in the dynamic mode of actual history.

Contemporary followers of Kierkegaard have developed his concept of the creative choice into a logic of existence which presents a special challenge in its application to the facts of messianic history. One of the most complete and lucid of these developments is that of the Italian Existentialist philosopher, Nicola Abbagnano. Utilizing the work of Heidegger and Jaspers, yet maintaining a studied independence of both of these thinkers, Abbagnano offers certain refinements and advancements of the existential rationale that are highly provocative and relevant to our present purpose. Particularly is this true of the manner in which, according to his analysis, the existential choice unites the past with the future.

This less well known exponent of Existential thought, Abbagnano, speaks (in the French of his interpreter, Georges Rageth) of the *"welding (soudure)* of a future situation which is undetermined in its possibilities, but which *ought* to be," with an initial situation accruing from the past; and he gives to this welding of past and future the (Italian) name of *Struttura,* or structure. This term, he indicates, "expresses the nature of the existential act in respect of its being problematical and uncertain. Structure effects the unity of past and future, though a decision which places in the future the significance of the past."[7] "In the decision which constitutes the 'structure,' a man really identifies himself with the possibility which his choice represents. He realizes himself in the choice of this possibility which he makes his own." Having recognized the possibility which is constitutive of his own personality, he "possesses himself entirely." In so doing he fulfills his "destiny."

The choice of this major possibility of one's life, Abbagnano continues, fixes those choices which follow. Thus it eventuates that the structure of the basic decision connects with the "transcendent possibility which corresponds to the final form of our being."[8]

There is no realization of one's essence apart from the "risk" involved in the major decision. An intensity of moral compulsion accompanies the choice by which one becomes himself. He is accepting himself as he joins the future to *his* past. "I ought to be what I have been, I ought to be in the future what really I have always been. The subjugation of the future to the past is the constitution of the past in the future." This subjugation or reduction of the future and this new constitution of the past form a simultaneous act which Abbagnano calls the "storicita" (historicity) of one's existence. It is the "continuity," of Kierkegaard's version of the existential choice. It is the present situation which, the Italian writer says, "defines me and limits me in my actual choice and forces me to be myself."[9]

In another article, under his own name and in an English translation, this philosopher amplifies certain of the above points. He introduces the thought of a careful retrospection in the life of the individual, as he observes: "But man cannot move towards the future without taking into consideration his past. The actualization of himself in the future is connected with the research of his true past. He must be and will be in the future that which he really has been."[10] This is the historicity of existence.

With regard to the "task" which one's decision presents, Abbagnano writes: "But an effective engagement of the ego towards itself and towards others is always the determination of a *task* . . . it is the recognition of a precise task which demands the concentration and utilization of all one's capacities."[11]

Even a cursory examination will show that these ideas reveal the highest degree of relevancy to the messianic career of Jesus. To the facts of His decision and of His historical situation and effect, an unparalleled application of this existential logic can be made. Nowhere else is there to be seen a total life-decision so impressive as that of Christ. He represents the ultimate illustration of what it is to make one solitary choice which predetermines all others; of accepting the "task" which His major decision has constituted, and of putting Himself wholly and unreservedly into it; of identifying Himself with, and making His own, the unique "possibility" that the messianic history affords; and thus actually placing in the future the significance of the prophetic past; His inescapable compulsion to be that which in the singleness and depth of His messianic consciousness He has always been; His knowing the dread, agony, and awful "risk" of the cross; and the most real "historicity" of the manner in which He welds past and future into a "structure" which is not only that of His personal decision but of the fullness of the historical process as well.

The decisive propositions of the Existential Christology, by which its rational cogency may be directly and unambiguously assessed are these: Personal being issues from the existential act of choice. It is not a *state* but a realization of *existence* through moral decision. In this decision the individual produces his own essence. The personal essence which the historic Christ has realized and in which He has fully established Himself is the *proper essence of the living God* by virtue of the fact that His decision and action coincide completely with the purpose and activity of God Himself. Because He has taken upon Him God's own "history," and made Himself one with the total dynamic of messianic occurrence (not for one "life-time" but for its entire course), because, in a word, He has in His decision *actually* become God in history, and maintained this vital identity in the consciousness of His authentic destiny, we may with realism and scientific justification affirm that Christ is God.

If He had undertaken to transform the idea of Christ into actual history and had never, in His own personal effect, approached even near to the prior stature of this symbol (as was true of some who were pretenders to the messiahship)— that is to say, if He had failed to incorporate this process and control it with a tremendous and novel expression of it—it would have to be said of Him that He was no more than human. But because He chose to execute the total plan of God in history and has succeeded not only in maintaining this process but also in exalting it beyond all human calculation, it becomes evident existentially that He is God as well as man. The divine tendency of history, from the moment of Christ's decisive engagement with it, has not collapsed but on the contrary has advanced with new and undiminishing vitality. Momentous factors (the Resurrection, the new experience of the Holy Spirit, the singular organism of the Church, the Christian orientation of time, the altered structure of the moral consciousness) arose in consequence of His personal appropriation of an investment in the messianic history.

A man is what he chooses to be; this man chose to be God. Not because He does God's work, but because He does it totally He proves His full divine identity. One is limited in one's being only by one's possibility. Here is one individual who is confronted with, and who makes His decision in reference to, unlimited possibility. The realization of the unlimited possibility of God is the product of the incomparable choice and actual vocation of Jesus Christ.

In the manner in which He binds past and future together in the unity of His central purpose and makes every historical movement tributary to Himself, Christ is manifestly the "complete fact" that the modern philosophy of the organism envisions.

J. S. Bixler has written concerning the nature of Whitehead's "actual occasion": "In an act of concrescence each event receives the past and it achieves its own subjective aim by the way it envisages future possibility."[12] This idea is superlatively fulfilled in the mission of Christ in the connection which He forms between a past which is uniquely meaningful and a future which cannot escape its impress.

It should be kept in mind that there is another factor in the existence of Jesus which even His decision, for all its historical and metaphysical importance, must not be allowed to conceal. And that is the fact that He stood at the juncture of a unique opportunity. If it can be said that He was the only person who by reason of His consciousness of mission and other spiritual prerequisites could assume the messianic role, it can also be said that from the historical standpoint only this particular time and situation could serve for the climax of the historico-tensional process. There doubtless are an infinity of reasons why some other individual could not have been the historic Christ, but one very sufficient reason is that providence does not make available to every man the possibility of a role which calls for the one and only messianic framework which history affords. The record of the actual Christ is that of one man in a unique position—a man possessed, moreover, of a unique address to that particular situation.

ASPECTS OF THE DEITY OF CHRIST

We have seen that Jesus' eschatological role is basic to the idea of His essence; so that apart from the world process there can be no valid conception of His deity. His *becoming* God within time is the "Christological" condition of His being God eternally. This is true not only because of the nature of historical existence but also because of the conceptual and dogmatic distinction which maintains between "God" and "Christ." It is of the essence of the idea of "Christ" that He is the *historical* representation of God. The actual Messiah can be both Christ and God only by being *God in history*. And this fact of God in history, if it is to be anything but a mere abstraction, must involve His existential participation in the actual process. He must really *become* God in the world.

The Word *became* flesh and dwelt among us. The striking converse is: A man *became* God and rose above us!

Christ's essence, although in an historical and temporal aspect it is realized in connection with His messianic decision, nevertheless assumes an absolute character in respect of the total relations through which He is equated with the transcendent and eternal God. This important fact, which is amenable both to the existential logic of history and to the necessities of an effective Christian dogmatic, provides the solution to a number of Christological problems.

First, the existential interpretation satisfies the demand of various types of religious realism for a human, historical Christ. His full participation in the actual emotions of the situation into which He came, His incomparable sympathy with human need, the profound tension of His vocational choice and of a subsequent career in which He endured "such contradiction of sinners against Himself," all these add up to a pulsating and "pathetic" humanity. At the same time His special messianic character is no less fully historical in view of its far-reaching relational and processive constitution. To say that this man was the Christ, in the full meaning of this theological term and in a way that is more than commensurate with the prophetic expectation and ideal, is in the light of the pertinent history as scientific as any judgment embracing a great complexity of facts can be. To say that He is God is still to be in the most meaningful relation to these same facts. And these facts—the facts of a Christian interpretation of history—are in themselves capable of furnishing the material of the most satisfactory and inclusive description of the living God.

As we have demonstrated earlier, one would not be in an untenable position if one were to say, in view of the whole pattern of historico-tensional occurrence, that "Christ" is even more historical than "Jesus." In the same system of actual relations the Christ who extends beyond "Pontius Pilate" enters more deeply into the texture of historic event than the Jesus who is, to be sure, the vital and controlling center of this total influence. This distinction, though it should not be pressed so far as to suggest a disruption of the essential unity that exists here, is the distinction which we earlier enunciated, between the "historical" and the "archaeological" Jesus. The "historical," as we can now see, includes the influence and interpretation, the projection and continuation of His original impulse, in a way that goes beyond those bare facts that a merely archaeological investigation might be able to recognize. Yet in a deeper sense, and in the truest theological perception, the historic Jesus and the historic Christ are one. The teacher from Nazareth and the Word that was made flesh are equally and integrally historic. His Resurrection is as deeply grounded in true historicity as His observance of the Passover. His presence in the upper room is as real as His prayer in Gethsemane or His sermon on the mount.

The existential facts which we have exhibited are not contrary to the idea of the *pre-existence* of Christ. They only place this concept in a different relation. His essential oneness with God entails the inferential doctrine that in this transcendent connection, which is not one of boundary but of coincidence through decision, and in the light of the whole of His messianic reality, this Christ was "in the beginning" as St. John expresses it, "with God" and "was God." The Christ who, from the relative standpoint of a definite moment in time, really establishes Himself as God through the most tense and authentic decision, is from the standpoint of eternity, God. The historic Christ is eternally God.

The tension between the temporal and the eternal remains, however, and is not rationally dissolved, in this existential Christology. Though the absolute references can be established as indicated, there are in this dynamic view of the reality of Christ certain factors which will not allow it to relapse into a static, substantialist conception. The entire tendency of this method is away from the thought of a divine "nature" whose abstractly conceived qualities occasion end-less irrelevant, unreal, and essentially irreligious construc-tions.

An example of this ever-present tension, is in the fact that the divine being of Christ cannot be understood as a reality that corresponds to any given moment in the experience of the observer. No single instant in time is coextensive with His being, and if we imagine that He exists in our cognitive mo-ment, we are misled as to the true character of the historical existence of Christ. Though He is personally equivalent to God in the overall view and in His actual historic comprehen-siveness, Christ does not exist in the isolated moment.

The reason for this assertion is that only that which has a history and continues in historic relationship is real. It can-not be said that Christ is God at any single instant because this "instant" itself does not exist. It is only an abstraction from the vital stream of historic occurrence. As such it is allied to those broader abstractions which it logically fosters, such as qualitative essence, nature, and objective immutabil-ity. The real is not divisible into instants. If you take, for ex-ample, an instantaneous concept of a tree, in any season of its life and at any moment, your conceptual grasp will not be a whole tree and it will not be a real tree. Its history, its use of time, will be omitted in this temporal "cross section" and the real will be falsified and lost. It is a tree in which the sap will never rise and on whose ideal branches no leaves will ever grow.

A single instant of a phonograph record yields only silence. Of the shortest conceivable journey one instant cannot repre-sent progress. So everywhere in the sphere of the actual, mo-tion and sequence are necessary components. If we extract a moment from life, it is death. A moment even in the exalted life and being of Christ is nonexistent. It is only in the con-summative aspect, in the actual fullness of history and in that reference in which He transcends history, that He *is* God. But in this ultimate reference there is no thought of a qualitative essence or of anything else that reflects the nature of the inanimate object.

The physical and mathematical moment is abstraction and non-being. The *existential moment* is a very different matter, and is in relation both to history and to absolute being. At this organic and original moment of decision, which is at once universally related and wholly transcendent, we may affirm that Christ is indeed God. This is so for all time, and for eternity, but not for the speculative moment which is severed from time and which has to do not with eternity but only with the dead past.

Certain possible criticisms of the Existential Christology may be answered similarly on the basis of these fundamental principles, which, unlike traditional metaphysics, take fully into account both the historical and the transcendent aspects of the Person of Christ. If it is asked whether this processive interpretation does not tend to deify *becoming* as opposed to being, the answer is forthcoming that the Existential view is careful to deify neither becoming nor being. It magnifies becoming as the category most agreeable to the reality of history, but it goes beyond this idea to a concern for the transcendent area in which the process receives its motivation and ground of meaning. This latter, we hold, is the ultimate reality of God, which cannot be defined either in terms of becoming or of being, but which eludes all categories except those which are suggested by the character of the historic Christ. This is not merely to say that the divine reality is in a class by itself. It is to say that God transcends "class" and category altogether. There is nothing like God but God Himself and, as the Gospels testify, Jesus Christ whom He has sent.

If this philosophy makes much of becoming, it is not to apotheosize this category, but to employ it in the discovery of world meaning. Becoming and *existence* are not God, but they are in relation to God with an immediacy which the static categories of the ancient naturalism do not possess. The process and structure evinced here are not Deity, but they are the effective *sign* of Him.

In reply to the possible criticism that this organismic theology represents Jesus' identification with God as being an agreement of His *will* rather than one of essential *being,* so that this modern doctrine would amount only to a sophisticated form of the Nestorian heresy, we may point out that the character of His unique messianic decision is such, in the act itself and in the totality and ultimacy of its connections, that it secures an existential constitution of His Person, in which He makes Himself One with the being of God. It is not simply that in some "spiritual" manner He *agrees* with God. Through a singular act of cosmic and infinite import by which He encompasses the entire extent of what is morally real and spiritually possible, and so constructs His own essence, He reveals Himself to be God.

In the historical, rather than the speculative sense; in the mood of open affirmation, and not strict definition; in the involvement of personal awareness, as against the fiction of impersonal detachment; in faith, but not without reason; in the sphere of the coincidence of knowledge and worship— the Christ of the New Covenant is to be equated with the God of creation and providence.

With this metaphysical interpretation of the center of the messianic process, which has amounted to a rational exploration of the unique *interiority* of this event, we have completed the second of the two principal stages of our Christological presentation. This study purports, then, to have demonstrated: (1) the uniqueness and total meaningfulness of the messianic structure, on the horizontal level of history; and (2) the existence of a vertical dimension, at the center of this structure, in which the evidence of the deity of Christ becomes specific in the logic of an existential ontology.

The discussion which follows is in the nature of a more varied interpretation of these two facts as they are seen to constitute an effective knowledge of God.

7

The Knowledge of God

> ". . . the religious experience without the vision of history would be empty, the historical event without the religious experience blind."—H. WHEELER ROBINSON [*Redemption and Revelation*, p. 16]

A significant aspect of the modern development of religious thought is the manner in which it has tended to divest itself of one standard of authority after another, as it has continually shifted the direction of its theological interest and confidence. It is as if the central concepts of the Gospel had clothed themselves rather quickly during the early centuries with an extensive and heavy covering of authoritative ideas, only to surrender these principles more gradually in a later period.

The metaphysical program by which the Church integrated its message with the thought life of the Hellenic and Roman world, and out of which came the great theological definitions of the Ecumenical Councils, entered largely into this process. But it seems clear that the particular principle of authority which emerged from this era to exercise the largest influence during the whole of the Middle Ages was that of the "Church" conceived as an absolute institution.

This idea lost its priority (except with the Roman Church)

at the time of the Reformation, and from the sixteenth century until the present there has continued this "peeling off," as of one layer after another, of the historic envelope of the idea of Christian authority. The principle of the Church was supplanted momentarily by a powerful combination of the "Word of God" and the "Holy Spirit," but subsequently, and with far too general an effect, by the "Bible" much less dynamically conceived. Afterwards, as the "acids of modernity" gradually reduced the notion of the peculiar authority of the Bible, the authoritarian principle attached itself to more restricted aspects of the Christian heritage. Particularly as the theological dogmas which accompanied biblical absolutism decayed, there came to be a strong emphasis upon such partial, but ostensibly very historical, factors as the life of Jesus interpreted in the "progressive" vein of moral idealism, and in the narrower aspect of His being the mystical means of the "Christian's communion with God." Finally even these residues of a thoroughly liberal and generally superficial historicism were thrown out by the eschatological and dialectical theologies of the twentieth century.

The effect of this, in the light of the present investigation, is that with these various authorities and former theological referents out of the picture, it is thrust upon us now that we have once more the original facts and experiences of biblical history as our effective referent. It is "once more" because this is the position of privilege in which the primitive church itself stood in the brief period before the historical envelope began to crystalize in ways that obscured this original reference. This awareness of the original history of biblical occurrence as theological referent is a circumstance of extreme importance to modern Christian thought. It means a new beginning and the opportunity for an interpretation that will be careful to maintain the emphasis where it ought always to be—in the basic facts themselves and in a genuinely historical mode of interpretation. To these facts, accordingly, and to a further illustration of the manner in which they constitute the substructure of an actual knowledge of God we return.

THE SPECIAL EVENTS OF BIBLE HISTORY AS THE
MATERIAL OF WORLD-UNDERSTANDING

We have seen that the central events of history are not a mere linear sequence, but a movement which has breadth and community of vital historical relations exhibiting the character of process. Viewed in their wholeness, these events present a structure of history.

All events, both large and small, near and remote, crucial and tributary, are involved in this process; but the structural aspect of this most significant "grouping of occasions" is best seen in certain major events. These are reconstructed from the point of view of the period of the Exodus in the Old Testament, from that of the post-Resurrection experience of the disciples in the New Testament, and later (by projection) from the standpoint of the final consummation of Christ's Kingdom at the end of history.

These events are totally concrete and yet possessed of such a special character in their historical connection that they become universal events. Each of them is, in the sense of Goethe's description, a "concrete universal." Which is to say that one must be reconciled to the paradox which they invariably offer to the philosophical historian. The modern reader is acutely aware of this difficulty as he is impressed with what are on the one hand localized happenings of a particular national history, and on the other hand far-reaching arch-events which claim to be indispensable to the whole of the philosophy of history. Symbolic in their expression and yet wholly actual, they are the most potent of historical motives.

It is inevitable that the Aristotelian mind should encoun-

ter in these biblical facts an "offense," a "scandal" such as
that with which the Greeks were first shocked in the testimony
of the specific God of Abraham, of Isaac, and of Jacob. These
events include the call of Abraham, the election of Israel and
the conclusion of the Covenant, the Exodus, the giving of the
Law, the conquest of Canaan, the establishment of the kingdom of David, the captivity and return, the prophetic promise
of messianic salvation, the coming of Christ, His death, His
Resurrection and Ascension, the advent of the Holy Spirit
at Pentecost, the birth of the Christian Church, its historic
ministry of witnessing, the consequent shaping of the Christian era, the realization of Judgment, and the final establishment of the Kingdom of God in its perfection.

The total series of historical events, of which the above are
the most salient, has a double significance. Its philosophic effect is to complete the central category which is best fitted to
interpret the word of experience. This is important in that it
makes theology once more relevant and indispensable to all
the sciences of humanity and of nature. For, as we have indicated, the category of event does not receive its full elucidation in any other field than that of Christian history and its
interpretation. Here it has its widest system of relations and
effects. Here only does it attain that capital stature which a
philosophical category demands.

But, though this rather technical and methodological consideration is of much importance to philosophy in general,
in its quest of a principle of integration, the second significance of the Christian world-pattern is of far greater moment
to theology and to the religious experience of people. This
is a much more immediate and practical effect and it amounts
to the revelation of God in history.

Central as they are to the whole community of cosmic
occurrences, these events of biblical and Christian history are
in such a position, and consequently in such a light, that it
is not possible to view them as abstract or in any sense self-

contained. They are pre-eminently events which are in the nature of purposive *actions,* the coincidence of event and personal agency being complete in them and pointing, with a compulsion stronger than that of logic, to a sufficient Actor whose will they must express. In such events, in the light of this purposive unity, we see not God Himself but the activity of God, which is utterly significant with regard both to His reality and to His character. The structure of biblical events is not the ultimate being of God but the unmistakable sign of Him in the broad manifestation of His purpose, the basis in history of His revelation of Himself.

It is not our intention to imply that this historical foundation, which is given in the *intuition of total form,* is itself the full reality of Revelation. Revelation is complete only when it becomes fully personal—"existential," if one prefers this term—and realized in the super-scientific area of faith and direct experience of God. The farthest side of Revelation cannot be construed by philosophy. No human category is definitive of God. He is neither substance nor idea nor event. He is only God. To say that He is idea, or thing, or process or anything conceivable in the realm of sub-personal being, is essentially to worship graven images. God is really nothing but God, which is the loftiest and most accurate definition of Him that is possible, the only judgment about Him that is in the last analysis scientific.

But within the human sphere it is the divine event, rather than any concept of substance, which is the actual approach to Him and the channel through which He makes Himself known. Hence our concern with history and with science. Recognizing that these disciplines are able to deal with Revelation only on its rational plane, and that the knowledge of God in its fullness does not lie within reason, we also recognize that it is in real *relation to* reason (because the world is God's world and history is meaningful) and that a very great advantage is served by ascertaining what this historical revelation is. To take the opposite view is to question whether all of life is significant, and to deny God's real immanence. We are so constituted as reasonable beings that, what we feel and believe, we must try to see in relation to fact, else our belief ceases to be authentic, and psychologically and socially effective. Erich Frank states it: "Faith must come to terms even with the opposing truths of scientific and practical reason, in which we trust in our everyday existence; it is the function of philosophy to strive toward the solution of this antinomy."[1] The task of reason is not completely to explain Revelation, but to locate it with reference to what is known and to incorporate the rational sector which it does possess within the total of real knowledge.

Moreover, it would be erroneous to suppose that the particular events which we have named are the only ones which constitute the historical side of Revelation. These major events become Revelation only when they are grasped in their actual community with the host of lesser historical occasions and conditions which surround them. It is the *totality* of this group-sequence which lays the ground of divine Self-disclosure, and this, it is very important to note, only when it includes those human facts which emerge (mainly in the fabric of Scripture) as the *reaction* on the part of the historical life of the chosen community to the special events which God has initiated in the world. These two factors, the totality of biblical event and the validity of the human reaction as a natural component of this whole, are supremely requisite to Revelation and must be considered together. Revelation is really revelation and response.

To perceive the meaning of the biblical structure as a whole is to make a beginning in the experience of Revelation. And it is a beginning which from the standpoint of the philosophic mind is of enormous importance, inasmuch as it constitutes the scientific method in theology. For this perception, or historical intuition, is a direct experience of *knowing*, and, though it is not equivalent to the complete "religious" experience of Revelation that is possible for any individual regardless of his degree of philosophical maturity, it is scientifically valid and effective in the same direct manner in which sensory perception is effective through the eyes and ears. Despite the vastness and complexity of this historical *object* (using the term in an epistemological rather than in an ontological sense), its perception is in principle characterized by the same *immediacy* and *givenness* which one experiences in common life in becoming aware of the particular arrangement of, let us say, a flower garden, an art museum, or a flight of wild geese. This broad historical prehension has not only directness, but also an intuitive device similar to that of ordinary sensory impressions, namely, the grasp of an intelligible *pattern* in the object. We shall not repeat here, but only allude to, the discussion of the intimate connection between form and meaning in chapter two.

It was shown that the necessity of the *wholeness* of the historical grouping lies in the fact, at once psychological and epistemological, that meaning accrues essentially to *forms,* and it is only the whole which presents an entirely significant form. This is the insight which we owe to the school of *Gestalt* investigators such as Wertheimer, Köhler, and Koffka; and in making this application of their thought to the data of theology we have developed a direct principle of rationality in a field where it has not heretofore been applied. Its advantage to the philosophy of religion is in the fact that it establishes a knowledge of "God in history" which is immediately and fully empirical. This historical knowledge, for all its significance to every science which claims human relevance, is but the broad threshold to that profounder knowledge of God which in the language of Christianity is called Revelation. But as a rationally circumscribed base it will insure the character of science to a very large segment of the knowledge-plus-faith entity which is Revelation.

THE LIMITATION, AND CONSEQUENT DEFINITION,
OF KNOWLEDGE

The intuition of total form is a non-discursive type of knowing in relation to primal religious facts and is not subject to the Kantian limitations of pure reason, by virtue of the fact that it is not "pure reason" at all but an original historical reason which calls for no other schema than its own immediate intuition of structure. In relation to its intended matter (epistemological object) it has no need of any hierarchy of "forms of the understanding," as in Kant's very Newtonian mechanism of the reason, because its design is not abstract and it achieves its knowledge directly from the facts themselves. To be sure, it does not grasp the "thing-in-itself" any more than does Kant's ordinary perception of objects, but it does accomplish all that knowledge can ever aspire to do—it does acquire an assurance concerning the object, an impression of character, in this instance a conviction of the agency of God in history. The knowing subject is *in relation* to the "Thing-in-itself," which is the transcendent Actor of the universe. The subject knows God without either being God or being subjectively equal to Him. It appears that Kant did not realize that the *idea* of knowing the thing-in-itself is an impossible one. To know the thing-in-itself would be to experience the object absolutely, that is, wholly *out of relation*—which amounts to a theoretical identification of the knower with the thing-in-itself, a confused transition from the matter of knowing to that of being. It is true that we do not know any object absolutely; but it does not follow from this that we do not know the object *really*.

The business of knowledge is simply to know the "thing" —not the thing-in-itself. The "in itself" aspect of the object is a primal integrity of the "other" which to you and to me must remain absolutely inviolable, whether the object is a "little flower in a crannied wall" or the Eternal God. There is as much of metaphysics as of poetry in the familiar lines of Tennyson in which he broods over the mystery of a wayside flower and declares that if he knew it altogether he would be as God.

The real effect of Kant's proof is not that we cannot know the thing-in-itself, but that we cannot by rational dialectic or otherwise know it *absolutely*, which is to *be* it. Having recognized this, we are in position to note that the one really incontestable proof which Kant does achieve is that we cannot ever know God as a *thing* among other things, an object after the order of comprehensible this-worldly objects. After the great critic of Koenigsberg, we will know Him as God or not at all. But, to know is to stand in a relation of significance. Apprehension, not ultimate penetration, is knowledge.

THE FALLACY OF A NON-RELATIONAL, POSITIVISTIC ANALYSIS OF HISTORICAL FACTS

It is becoming increasingly clear that the truth of Christianity has suffered disastrously from a kind of analysis which at the very point of its thoroughness has missed the true locus of meaning. Concerning this type of science it has been justly said, "But they have only analyzed the parts and overlooked the whole, and indeed their blindness is marvellous."[2] In the sphere of Revelation as in Wordsworth's sanctum of nature it is "murder to dissect."

Not only must the totality of the historical object be involved if one is to be impressed with its truth, but there must be on the subjective side a comparable totality of *response*. It is an act of knowing into which the whole of one's person must enter, including the emotional and volitional as well as the simply intellectual response, since elements of evaluation, decision, and deepest personal concern are present. Thus the judgment of C. S. Lewis is true of historical Revelation when he says, " . . . while in other sciences the instruments you use are things external to yourself (things like microscopes and telescopes), the instrument through which you see God is your whole self."[3] A judgment upon the truth of Revelation is accordingly a judgment as to the most valid whole-response which it is possible for one to make in the variegated range of human knowledge and experience. And such a judgment can never be devoid of an existential character. The Revelation as a whole compels me in the entirety of my being to give answer to it in the one way or in the other.

THE DISTINCTION BETWEEN FACT AND HISTORY

The term *history* connotes a human and experiential addition to simple *occurrence*. Occurrence is the unknown heart of the world fact. History is a basic stage of its interpretation, for it is a telling of how the fact has touched other events, especially in human lives, and of what it has begun to mean. *History* is based on the Greek "to know," and it is therefore a description of the relations that exist between one event and another. The word *story*, which is the popular synonym of history, has its equivalent in the verb form, to "relate." When we relate an incident we not only "tell" it, but in the telling interpret its connections. History is thus related fact.

History deals with the unanalyzable centers of occurrence. In themselves they mean nothing. But they are the essential conditions of all meaning. As the hole in the center of a wheel is nothing, except in relation to the axle which passes through it, so these intersections become "something" by virtue of the historical relations which inform them. Especially is this true of those great discontinuities which are the central events of Revelation. These unexplainable but all-important occurrences of which the Resurrection is the most representative, appear as *perforations* in the actual continuum ("natural order") of world happenings.

When we think of this entire system of events as being bounded by transcendence, the view of the world of experience that is suggested by these unfathomable events of biblical history is, accordingly, one that we may express in the formula: an *irregular bounded continuum*. Its irregularity is in these major perforations which, in an oversimplified theology, would be regarded as wholly "supernatural." The real facts compel us to see in these perforations both organic and super-organic characteristics. Yet they are not basically unlike those more common and limited events which reveal at their core, also, only the blank "nothing" of the unrelated fact.

The Bible represents the stage at which actual occurrence is converted into historical and religious meaning. This interpretational function gives to the Bible an importance that is in proportion to that of the singular events which it relates.

The most fundamental aspect in which Bible history carries on its function of interpretation is that in which it reveals the pattern which lies in the events themselves. This is prior to the verbal message, or "propositional" truth which is the scriptural text. This pattern is the structural formation of history. Like an arrow it points toward that *event* which is the terminus of the time of preparation and the beginning of the new age of the Kingdom of God in Christ. So distinct is this funnel-like structure of history from the plane of relatively unexceptional occurrence around it that it provides an angle, or principle of formal contrast, with ordinary history that will be maintained no matter how far this plane should be extended. This mathematical analogy, which may serve to illustrate the nature of this special history, is in the fact that a perpendicular of only one inch will still serve to erect a true angle over an unbroken plane even when the latter has reached to millions of miles. In this fashion, the uniqueness of the biblical sequence of events is completely guaranteed through its angle of revelatory elevation.

To all suggestions that an event in time cannot have absolute significance, and that a few thousand years are as nothing in a stellar universe, and so on, there is the irrefutable answer that an absolute sign has been given within finite history in the unique configuration and transcendent reference of biblical events. And the logic of this contention is such that the notion of a billion light-years does not affect it.

More basic, and metaphysically more conclusive, than any of its verbal formulations, is this actual sign-message of Bible history. It is the *revealing of what is* prior to its translation into words, or even into thought, save the most elemental structure of the mind's intuition of the primal form. The deepest truth, as some are now telling us, is in this pre-verbal stage. Heidegger, for instance, is saying that truth is the "uncovering" of what is. Its real seat therefore is not in a correct proposition and its correspondence with a fact or a thing (though this is also truth) but in the open wholeness in which things are when man lets them be what they really are.[4] Truth is the "uncovering of the things that are *within the whole*." This conception of a "letting be open" of what *is,* leads Heidegger to the assertion that, *"The essence of truth is freedom."*[5]

A new appreciation of biblical truth arises from the recognition of the basic and arresting pattern which the history *as such* lets come to light. The verbal and propositional level of the truth of Scripture will mean much more when it has been viewed in this incomparable setting. It will be known then to be the voice of a unique concretion of world meaning.

The most outward phase of the biblical community of events is the text of Scripture. In this literary surface composed of words and grammatical propositions, the meaning which inheres in the original events becomes explicit and detailed. The spiritual import of the whole structure is expressed here, and, above all, this spiritual meaning is articulated in the message of the Person who is the controlling center of the historical process. Christ's words possess a unique authority that is in keeping with His grasp and disposition of the divine tendency within history.

The special relation of the literary aspect of Scripture to the knowledge of God, and reasons for regarding the Bible as actual Revelation rather than as a mere record of God's revelatory activity, require separate treatment and will be the subject of the following chapter. The important thing to notice at this point is that the verbal enunciation of biblical events is a part of the system of meaningful relations which begin at the pre-interpretational level of dynamic structure.

There is that in the biblical events which draws the mind of the researcher into an area of knowing experience that goes both beneath and beyond the significance of their literary formulation. The experience tends to be not a mere "knowing about," but a profound spiritual "engagement with," the event, in which the reflecting subject feels that he is more grasped *by* the historical truth than he is in the position of grasping it. Knowledge thus becomes spiritual communion. From the standpoint of the phenomenology of religion, G. van der Leeuw describes this type of historical comprehension as follows:

> In other words: the more deeply comprehension penetrates any event, and the better it "understands" it, the clearer it becomes to the understanding mind that the ultimate ground of comprehension lies not within itself, but in some "other" by which it is comprehended from beyond the frontier. Without this absolutely valid and decisive comprehension, indeed, there would be no understanding whatever. For all comprehension that extends "to the ground" ceases to be comprehension before it reaches the ground, and recognizes itself as a "becoming understood." In other

terms: all comprehension, irrespective of whatever object it refers to, is ultimately religious: all significance sooner or later leads to ultimate significance.[6]

If this is true of events generally, it must be particularly true of those which, prior to our cogitation upon them and quite independently of us, are in a special relation to the transcendence in which they are enacted. To penetrate to the heart of such events is to be in touch with that which is no longer an object but divine reality.

THE KNOWLEDGE OF GOD AS SUPER-RATIONAL

We have come now to the second type of experience based upon the revelatory events of Bible history, and one which in its religious value is more advanced than that experience of historical and literary understanding which we have identified with the interpretational phase of biblical occurrence. We are referring now to the existential and fully spiritual experience to which the other contributes. This is the direct knowledge of God which transcends thought, or in which thought is a strictly subordinate element. This immediate experience of God neither knows Him as an object nor conceives Him as an idea. It simply encounters Him in His transcendence. Yet to this encounter it does bring that which it has learned on the interpretational level, and this gives coloring and spiritual content to man's experience of transcendence. It is extremely important that this fact be fully regarded. The contact with transcendence would be neutral and spiritually less valuable without the contribution of the prior interpretational stage.

Yet insofar as its character as an act of knowledge is concerned, it cannot be overstressed that this personal and existential experience of God is wholly distinct from the objective and ideational mode. It is in the "I-Thou" relationship of persons rather than in the "I-it" pattern of objective perception. For God is not an object but a self. This assertion involves a world of difference.

In my hand I hold a ball-point pen. It is an object. And it has all the usual character of objectivity. I control and use this ball-point. I understand it. I *own* it. Not only am I able to encompass the most significant of its actual relations and functions, and on the basis of this knowledge succeed in making the object serve my will, but I complete my domination of it, my real and conscious superiority to it, by claiming that it is mine.

My relation to God is the opposite of this. I do not "grasp" Him, either with my hand or with my mind, as I grasp this writing instrument. I certainly do not control Him, and the thought of *using* Him is repellent to all that I have rightly learned to think about Him. I do not own Him but am grateful to think that I am owned by Him, and this not in the sense of a "thing" but of a "child." There is given to me no possible means by which I could put myself in a position of relational superiority to Him. I cannot examine Him or understand Him because He is altogether too extensive for my reach. I can reach to Him but not around Him. I can perceive only that the logical direction is from me to Him and not from Him to me, so that when this natural fact is reversed I know that it is by virtue of His grace and not of my right that He should thus approach me. He is central. I am peripheral. He is the Thinker, I the thought.

We know God but never all of God. We cannot possibly comprehend Him, because this would be to *surround* His being with our idea. We can only *apprehend* Him with that partial knowledge which suggests contact rather than enclosure. Since there is always in our experience of Him an infinite *difference* as well as an actual *meeting,* one might employ the term *contrahension* to suggest this dialectical situation. To know Him is to realize this essential opposition as well as its gracious annulment in the religious act. Contrahension denotes both boundary and communication, impossibility and grasp.

By the same token we cannot really *conceive* of God, for here again the *con* suggests an encompassing of His being that is never attained in our actual knowledge of Him. We cannot throw any such circle of epistemological conquest around the living God. We can conceive of God only in respect of particular divine traits that have come into our experience, especially those that have been made known to us through the historic Christ. Our appreciation of the Person of Christ is at its fullest, however, not a concept but a communion. What we think of as our concept of God is, as Richard Kroner expresses it, not a true concept at all, but a "holy image."[7] The Ultimate which is God is not the "universal" of human logic.

Henry Adams says that when he entered Chartres Cathedral and tried to grasp the meaning of this great work of art, he found that it was so richly abundant that he had to content himself with feeling such a part of it as he could; for understand, he could not! This, raised to the "nth" degree, is the situation which prevails in our knowledge of God.

Our experience of Him, though it involves conceptual knowledge and fulfills it, is not conceptually produced. It is an existential attitude, to which the informational and the logical are entirely subordinate. It is a situation which, as Kroner significantly points out, "can never be construed or reconstrued by means of thought. It is a living situation which embraces the totality of the personal life. This totality can be analyzed by the intellect, but it cannot be rebuilt out of the analyzed elements."[8]

The existential can utilize the interpretational, but the latter unaided by something more basic than itself can never reach an authentic religious experience. God is not known by virtue of the idea but through the communication of the divine self.

It is the unique value of the Christian interpretation of both historical occurrence and personal existence, that it alone endows the existential consciousness with a fully *redemptive meaning*. An existential awareness of God is not in itself a saving experience. It may seem as close to fate and doom as to possibility and renewal. It is, in any case, the "still small voice" in the heart of the storm, the readiness to hear what God has to say, and perhaps an actual hearing— but the content of God's word in the existential situation depends upon ideas and moral experiences of God that must have gone before. The glory of the Gospel, existentially speaking, is that it informs the soul's most desperate moment with the illuminating and conquering precedent of the cross. It wrings from crisis a more than existential *hope*.

God cannot be wholly known because He is not, in the Latin sense of the term, an existent. He does not "stand out" (*existere*) for our observation and comprehension in the way that finite entities do. Instead of being a *particular*, thrust forward by some more basic and creative force, He is the ground of all particularity and the transcendence of all actuality. Our conceptual references to Him are but symbols of limited and varying worth.

Yet in one amazing instance, without negation of His infinity or any compromise of His perfect spirituality, He does particularize Himself in history, in the Person of Jesus Christ. There alone the living God "stands out" for man to see, and actually to understand, as the express image of the invisible God. In Him the knowledge of God is complete, as He fulfills the Promise and the perennial deep need of our humanity:

'Tis the weakness in strength, that I cry for! my flesh, that I
    seek

In the Godhead! I seek and I find it. O Saul it shall be
A Face like my face that receives thee; a Man like to me,
Thou shalt love and be loved by, forever: a Hand like this
    hand
Shall throw open the gates of new life to thee! See the Christ
    stand![9]

*   *   *   *   *

Let us summarize briefly before going to the subject of
Scripture and the place which it has in this view of Revelation. Omitting for our immediate purpose the particular find-
ings in regard to an Existential Christology, and thinking
only of the broader development—we have shown that the
historical intuition of the biblical sequence is itself a direct
and valid means of knowledge. This claim is vindicated by
a realistic epistemology which is similar to the current psychology of vital form, and which is possessed of a prehen-
sional rather than a discursive method. The term, *intuition
of total form*, represents the specific act of knowledge, and
the overall method may be called the historical reason. What
is known by this method is that a creative and purposive God
is at work in history. The uniqueness of the revelation of God
which the biblical sequence comprises is immediately grasped
in the peculiar *structure* of history as well as in a consideration of the principle source events. Its authority is one of concrete experience rather than abstract proof, and the psychological correlative of this authority is meaning.

The controlling center of the historical structure, to whom
the source events belong and in whom they are seen to exhibit peculiar depth, is the Person of Christ. He is Himself
the chief interpreter as well as the principal originator of the
revelatory events.

Beyond historical meaning, and yet in direct touch with it,
is the existential experience in which the knowledge of God
is essentially personal and "religious" as opposed to merely

intellectual. Interpretation, when it reaches the appropriate point, invests itself in this existential knowledge so as to make it Christian and redemptive. As the cross is the clarification of existence, so Jesus Christ is the fullness of the knowledge of God. Because of where He stands and who He is, it is God Himself who speaks when Christ translates historical event into living speech. And, as we shall confirm shortly, the words themselves are the actual continuation and fruition of the singular and world-altering events.

8

The Bible:
Confrontation and Communication

"The Bible . . . stands in a unique relation to some unique and supremely significant events."—JOHN KNOX [*Christ The Lord*, p. 69]

THE Scriptures of the Old and New Testaments are the record of the revelation which God has made of Himself through the central, distinctive development of events in which the shaping and meaning of history are found. The Scriptures are, however, much more than a "record" or testimony of this historic revelation. Because they participate vitally in the original revelatory events, we are justified in claiming that the Bible is itself Revelation.

There is a real sense in which the Bible is continuous with the historical structure and completes it in a manner in which the primal occurrence and relational sequence alone could not complete it. Scripture is the interpretational phase of men's concrete experiences of revelation in its more original and epochal sense. It is only in the Scripture that these events become fully religious; for it is only here that broad, spiritual meaning is joined to them, so as to make of them an actual "unveiling" of the foundational events.

To show that (1) the Bible *is* itself Revelation, not in an

139

abstracted "qualitative" sense but in the vital, processive sense indicated above, (2) to determine a more plausible context for the idea of the *authority* of the Christian Revelation, and (3) to provide a valid and realistic definition of the term *inspiration* as applied to the Bible, are the main objectives of this chapter.

The identification of Scripture with Revelation, which is entirely credible from the historical point of view, is in decided contrast not only with the "agnostic" attitude of those who for critical and "scientific" reasons have banished the idea of the authority of Scripture completely, but also with the view of a large and impressive segment of contemporary theology. This identification has been rendered particularly unfashionable during the years since Barth and Brunner made their immense impress upon the doctrine of Revelation. Recalling now the Barthian insistence that the Scripture is not the Word of God but only the paradoxical means of a Revelation which is nowhere identical with the written word, let us note how widespread this distinction between Scripture and Revelation has come to be, and see if one cannot detect the verbal inaccuracy and disagreement which it harbors.

Very few of the prominent writers who have been influenced by the dialectical theologians will part company with these authorities now on this point. They tend to follow the misleading half-truth that Brunner has typically expressed in the statement that "the word of Scripture is not in itself the word of God but of man, just as the historical appearance of the God-man is in itself that of a man."[1] A "fatal step," he says, is this of "regarding Scripture as true in itself, as revelation in itself . . ."[2]

Witness several outstanding British and American scholars. William Temple, for example, declares that "there is no such thing as revealed truth." "There are truths of revelation, that is to say, propositions which express the results of correct thinking concerning revelation; but they are not themselves directly revealed."[3] Dr. Temple holds, correctly, that revelation is given in historical events when the prophetic mind is present and able to appreciate and interpret their significance. Revelation results from "the coincidence of event and appreciation," and "its essence is intercourse of mind and event, not the communication of doctrine distilled from that intercourse."[4] But on the basis of these largely true and discerning observations he draws the, by no means necessary, inference that: "There is no imparting of truth as the intellect apprehends truth, but there is event and appreciation; and in the coincidence of these the revelation consists."[5] He seems to separate the cognitive element from Revelation entirely when he says, "What is offered to man's apprehension in any specific revelation is not truth concerning God, but the living God Himself."[6]

John Baillie similarly holds that "revelation consists neither in the dictation of writings nor in the communication of information, but in personal communion—the self-disclosure of a Personality."[7] But why associate so closely "dictation" and "information?" Surely the breakdown of a dictation theory of Scripture does not eliminate the meaningful aspect of Revelation. And why should the self-disclosing "Personality" be so loath to intimate some meaningful impression, some idea, of Himself?

George F. Thomas, in answer to the question, what is the *content* of Revelation, says, "It is not as dogmatists have said, articles of faith, propositions which state truths about God and His Will in final and unalterable words ... . God reveals *Himself*, not mere ideas about *Himself*."[8] And John Knox writes, "The Bible is not itself the revelation of God; it is the record or report of the revelation." And again, "For the Word of God is not a word at all (much less a vast number of words); it is an act." God is "not imparting truths about himself."[9]

These theologians are as one voice in taking the position

that Revelation must be *either* divine action *or* the word of
Scripture. The assumption is that there can be no community
between these two factors, as if God were determined to
have nothing to do with human intelligence; and this assumption is based uncritically upon Barth's deliberate ontological
separation of the Word of God from history. If our study has
shown anything at all, it has shown that God's acts are not
divorced from history but are the ground and texture of all
historical reality and specifically the source of Revelation.
What needs to be made explicit on the basis of this proposition, and underscored for all realistic theology, is that the
words of Scripture are themselves events in actual relation
to all other events in the biblical community. Words have
their place among the historical effects of these events of
Revelation in their human course. All that we have said
about the unity of fact and meaning applies here, to contro-
vert the Barthian position.

There is an element of truth in the point of view illustrated
in the above quotations. It is that the word of Scripture is not
an *absolute* word, and that the linguistic expression of God's
truth is not the most divinely *immediate* aspect of His Revelation. When God's self-disclosure assumes the conceptual
and propositional form, it is, in fact, involved in historical
and human relativity. Yet this does not preclude the idea that
the words and propositions of Scripture are a real and integral part of the Revelation.

It is not difficult to see how these current theologians have
drawn their inference that Scripture is not Revelation. They
found the traditional idea of Biblical authority permeated
by the categories of a substantialist philosophy. There is no
denying that in the past the equation of Scripture with Revelation has often gone hand in hand with a belief in its literal
infallibility based upon a qualitative concept of its revelatory
character. But the substantialist category is not essential to

our identification of Scripture with Revelation. In the dynamic mode it is still true that the Bible is Revelation, not simply in an instrumental, but in an actual, sense of a community of historical occurrence.

From the recognition that Scripture is not a "thing" and not a rational absolute, it does not follow that it cannot be identified, in the way of a vital historical connection rather than in an exhaustive sense, with the activity of God in which His Revelation of Himself primarily occurs. The theologians whom we have quoted are, in an opposite manner, victimized by the same absolutist fallacy which they have detected in the literalists. For these writers, in their objection to the substantialization of Scripture, employ a similarly abstract principle in denying revelatory character and content to it *entirely*. Their "is not" is as unhistorical and philosophically invalid as the over-generalized "is" of the qualitative literalists. Their refusal to regard Revelation *substantially* leads them erroneously to regard it *negatively*, so that in their view it comes to lack real historicity altogether. A personal communion with God in which *meaning* has no place, or an occurrence which does not extend to interpretation and reasonable witness, is a "wholly other" which actually nullifies the thought of an historic revelation.

The words of Scripture constitute the outer reflections, or to be more exact, outer re*verb*erations, of the same events which in the great epochs of the Bible begin as divine occurrence. The Revelation is not in the original occurrence alone (it could not be, for in some of the chief instances these are to the human observer totally unknowable) but in the relations which flow from these through historical action including ideation and speech. Spoken and written words are the human, vibrant fringe of God's events. His action within these words distinguishes them from ordinary human speech, even though they are the familiar words of ordinary discourse. Except for these and their terminal in the human consciousness there would be no Revelation, but only a primitive blind awe.

Take, for instance, the experience of Isaiah in the Temple "in the year that King Uzziah died." That God revealed Himself to this prophet no sympathetic student of religion can doubt. But what is this event apart from the emotion of the prophet's heart, his despair, his shame, his love, his new dedication, and the *words* through which his own Divine-human encounter has become the inspiration of countless others, a continuing reverberation of holiness through the centuries? And these words, redolent with divine action, are in the text of Scripture, joined indissolubly to the event, a revelation as authentic as any smoke and lightning of Sinai. Who made man's tongue, that God should not use it in the service of a Revelation that is for man's own sake as well as for God's glory! God is not only "numinous" and remote. He is also the Father, who first begot the Word in eternity, an event whose purpose was communion.

THE NATURE AND FUNCTION OF REVELATION

It is correct to say that Scripture is Revelation because it conveys the meaning and truth of Bible events. Revelation is a historical concept and not primarily a metaphysical one. Its object is to bring persons into a relation with what is metaphysical without being a metaphysical entity itself. It is essentially a bridge between the infinite and the historical. The Barthian opposition to the identification of Scripture with Revelation is based on a concept of Revelation as being somehow equivalent with God rather than the instrumental process of His making Himself known. It is true, as the dialectical theologians assert, that God reveals *Himself*; but it is not true (as they say) that the Revelation *is* Himself. In comparison with God Himself, Revelation must have a secondary and derived character, that of agency and expression.

In this we are in agreement, of course, with traditional theology, but with a profound difference. Whereas the basis of the traditional conception is substantialist, this concept is relational and functional, stressing God's activity and personality rather than the static quality of the product of revelation in its verbal form. But there is ample objectivity for this view in the reality of the history which Scripture encompasses, in the incomparably meaningful content of the literature, and in the super-human influence of God's Spirit as He gives form and character to the whole.

It is the nature of Revelation that it should not be absolute in the sense of manifesting the whole of God's reality, while it should be absolute in reference to other conceivable revelations and systems of truth. No man has seen God at any time and no word even (except the Living Word who is the Son) ever fully discloses Him. As Franz Werfel expresses it, "Not even the Deity can make the parables of His Being of equal rank and equal value to His Being Itself."[10] But if on the one side Revelation cannot be so absolute as to be equal to the whole being of God, there is also the compensating truth that Revelation implies a real accomodation on the part of God to the nature and need of man. One of the primary ideas in the term revelation is that of a *com*munication. The relation established in this process must extend *all* of the way to the human recipient of revelation. The initiative on the part of Deity is implied in such a manner as to exhibit His willingness to make an accomodation to the knowing capabilities of those whom He would reach. This is not at all unthinkable whenever God's immanence is allowed. The transcendence of God's own nature does not cancel the possibility of His making use of ideas or any other intramundane means, for that matter, to impart a knowledge of Himself to men. We are not to assume that God, because He is not idea, can have no relation to ideas.

Niebuhr puts this succinctly when he says,

> The finite world is not, because of its finiteness, incapable of entertaining comprehensible revelations of the incomprehensible God. The most important characteristic of a religion of revelation is this twofold emphasis upon the transcendence of God and His intimate relation to the world.[11]

Quite apart from our previous analysis of an event in its historical aspect, it should be observed that on the psychological and experiential level it is impossible to conceive of a communion with another person in which there is no intellectual content or real communication.

Revelation is the special historical activity by which God makes Himself known to man, not God Himself as ineffable, but God's expression in primal deed and in human reaction and interpretation. Only Scripture embraces the entire action of God's self-disclosure in both of these aspects and thus vindicates its claim to the title of Revelation. The Scriptural Revelation is a complex of which the conscious knowledge of God is an essential part, knowledge which is different from other knowledge in that it is specifically the knowledge *of God*, yet true knowledge because of the human goal of God's communication, and because of the continuity of this with all experience of knowing in the world.

The knowledge of God and the knowledge of truth concerning Him are not contradictory but are rather bound in a single reference to the original revelatory event. They are complementary and tend constantly toward unity. It is a question only of the degree of nearness to the divine initiation, a matter of relation, not of distinction. Yet such is the nature of this revelatory community that God is apprehended in its wholeness as well as in the super-rational area of its source. Without Scripture no such wholeness becomes effective. The historical necessity of the element of human response is the reason why Revelation cannot dispense with the written Word, or let its definition be severed from this conception. To say that Revelation is Scriptural is to say that it is genuinely historical. God might reveal Himself to angels or spirits without such an intelligible medium as Scripture, but we cannot imagine how even the Almighty could reveal Himself to men without some other vehicle than that of pure divine action.

As event and meaning are inseparable, so Revelation must join in one vital continuity the divine occurrence and the human response to it, the fact and the interpretation of it, the effective witness to it, in the actual *words* of Scripture. This insures that the text itself possesses a revelatory character and status. Only such a Revelation can at once preserve and incessantly renew the one "imperishable occasion" in which the meaning of history is manifest. The Scripture is the constant possibility of renewing the experience of the centrality of Christ's Person in the life of the individual as it is historically in the life of the world. It is, in the fine phrase of Stanley R. Hopper, the means of "re-creating the moment that has transfigured the world."[12]

Revelation is a matter of experience before it is a matter of record. Without the prior experience, the record would be insignificant and false. Nevertheless, the record, which is the scriptural witness, is an actual and indispensable phase of Revelation inasmuch as God continues to speak through this communicated Word.

THE INSPIRATION OF SCRIPTURE

An integral and historical view of Scripture is not in the least incompatible with a concept of divine Inspiration. In fact there is no idea which serves so well as that of Inspiration to account for the unique process by which the peculiar source-events of Scripture are fused with the whole body of interpretation which the Bible presents as its intelligible, surface aspect. There are at least two characteristics which set this biblical inspiration apart from that of other literature. They are (1) the radically distinctive influence of the events themselves upon the persons who recorded them, and (2) a providential supervision of the whole course of this interpretation in the interest of scriptural unity, a unity which coincides with that of history but which is made luminous and spiritually effective in the words of Scripture. In this community of interpretation (the word *system* is too intransigent for our use here) every idea is organically related to its Christian center in a way which transcends any possibility of historical accident, and which in some instances appears to transcend even the understanding of the writers of Scripture —as in the prophets of the Old Testament, whose concepts were moving steadily toward ever larger meanings.

The effect of the former of these two factors is to produce a spiritual *character* which is unique, and the effect of the latter is to bring about a *formal* (structural-schematic) separation from the generality of world history which is equally significant. Both of these singular historical influences are rightly attributed to the Holy Spirit. No other explanation will suffice for historical circumstances so extraordinary. What Archbishop Temple wrote about Revelation would seem to be even more applicable to *Inspiration*, conceived in this dynamic-historical manner. Seeing God in the whole of this spiritual affair Temple expressed His relation to it thus: "He guides the process; He guides the minds of men; the interaction of the process and the minds which are alike guided by Him is the essence of revelation."[13]

There are important points of divergence between this concept of Inspiration and that which inheres in the substantialist (orthodox) approach. From this relational point of view we no longer have reason to require that every particle of Scripture shall have the same absolute authority as that of the whole. The very concept of relation implies an objection to this "atomistic" manner of regarding Scripture, as does also a realistic impression of the nature of literature. A recognition of the *historical* character of the Sacred Writings constantly magnifies the consideration of perspective and weight.

The *motive* of those who will not relinquish the literal absolutism of Scripture (in reference to individual words and sentences) is basically sound and worthy of more Christian and scholarly respect than it receives in liberal quarters. It is not the motive but the science of this group which is at fault. The motive is primarily to determine an objective ground for the idea of the unique authority of the scriptural Revelation. With this aim the present writer and many others in various theological parties are in close agreement. The emptiness of the average "Liberalism" is that it has not had the discernment to see how entirely necessary from the standpoint of a Christian philosophy some such effect as this is.

THE LOGIC OF SUBSTANTIALIST INSPIRATION

What is the real method of the believer in verbal absolutism? And what is the logical necessity which usually compels him to deny the *naturalness* of the human instrumentation in Scripture, in favor, as he supposes, of what must be its invariable, uncompromised divinity? The literalist discountenances and distorts the human factor in Scripture because he has been able to find no other place than the *literary surface* of Revelation on which to erect a *formal principle* by which this Revelation may be adequately distinguished, metaphysically from what is not special Revelation. He is right in his grasp of the necessity of this formal principle. He is right also in his determination to find it within the historical entity of Scripture. He is mistaken only in his *location* of this principle, and the mistake has proved most tragic in the incalculable cost of the warfare between the spirit of science and the spirit of faith, as this conflict has developed in consequence of the Fundamentalist position.

The Christian thinker who is governed by the substantialist concept of the Inspiration of Scripture is not concerned primarily with the thought: "God must make no mistake!" (This is involved, but not essentially.) His major concern is: "This Word must be *different*—in its actual *quality*—from any other word." If the Revelation as a whole is divine and absolute, the quality of absoluteness must inhere in every fraction. (For is it not true that every atom of a lump of coal must be coal?) The test which the literalist imposes, accordingly, will be at the point of every separate word, and the criterion of the Scripture's differentiated quality must be the literal factual correctness of every proposition which it contains. Into this quality, thus abstractly conceived, no human or temporal imperfection must enter. Not only is the Word divinely given but it is also divinely received, to the virtual abrogation of the human factor and the historical vitality which is the concomitant of this factor.

Thus comes into existence a Scripture which must rate as infallibly in the role of natural science as in the sphere of the revelation of the character and saving purpose of the eternal God.

The solution of this paramount quandary of Protestant thought is to retain the logical function of this objective principle, a valid insight of the Fundamentalists, while making a revolutionary shift in its location, a change which is indicated by the nature of the facts involved and which is directed as to method by the position of these facts themselves. Whereas the substantialist tries to see in the quality of the Scripture's literal text a sign of its objective difference from all other types of information, and so grounds a standard of authority, our theology of history locates its formal principle with reference to the scriptural Revelation as a whole, in the specific *structure* which characterizes this Revelation with respect to its entirety and to its unity, a structure which is in itself a supremely effective sign of historical differentiation.

IMPLICATIONS OF THE HISTORICAL STANDARD

The first of several advantages gained by this strategic shift of the formal principle is that the *objectivity* of this principle now becomes empirical whereas in its employment by orthodoxy it has been entirely *a priori*. Here it is a self-assertive principle, whereas before it has had to be the object of faith. Faith is hereby released for a more spiritual service— to become faith in a message rather than in a mode, in the Revelation itself rather than in the theory of its inspiration. From this standpoint there obtains a real standard of reference, capable of verification through recourse to historical events. It is obvious that the theological effect of this shift, in its displacement of the problems of literal inerrancy, is a very major one.

The important thing about the text of Scripture henceforth is not that it should be an unalloyed demonstration of factual accuracy, but that it should be seen in relation to the whole of the unique community of Revelation of which it is a part, and thus have divine meaning. To have been wrought within the fabric of this whole, in the living process of which Scripture is the completion, is sufficient to establish the part as Revelation. This is the criterion: it participates in the meaning of the whole.

It is plainly encumbent upon us as Christians that we should dare to believe that the "Word became flesh." God has never expected us to believe that the Word became grammar!

As for the interpretation of Scripture, the part (verse or passage) is to be interpreted in relation to the center of this Revelation, which is the Mind of Christ. In some instances the single proposition may be in the nature of an ultimate deliverance, so immediate is its proximity to the Center, or to the Source, which is One with Him. In other instances the historical method will indicate a minor and indecisive relation to the larger truth which must serve as the court of judgment. Texts may be used as proof-texts only with the understanding that one text is not equal to another in proof or in the value of its truthfulness. The largest meaning will attach to the whole. But—and this is the beauty of Scripture—every word will be able to place one's feet in the way that leads to the perfect knowledge of God, and every part will bear the impress of His Spirit.

THE CANON OF SCRIPTURE

This discussion of the authority of the Biblical Revelation could not be completed, even in brief outline, without some reference to the concept of the boundary of Scripture which is involved in the history of the Canon. The boundaries of Scripture, in the sense of the Canon which lists its rightful "Books," are not to be thought of in the *absolute* manner of a substantialist metaphysic, but in the practical sense of historical determination. The general postulates of this dynamic theology as we have described it require what is in theory a fluid concept of the limits of Scripture, but what in reality becomes fixed, with a very high degree of historical finality.

This fixation has come about by virtue of the fidelity with which Christian experience (Christian men plus God) has tested the various books which were considered for and included within the Canon. But the significant factor is not the judgment of the Church to include these books while rejecting certain others, but that there was in them an intrinsic value which the Church could not but recognize in the main (we say "in the main" in deference to those books which were debatable—the fluid margin). This value of the canonical books resides in the books themselves in relation to the totality of the historical movement which has brought them into existence. The determination of the Canon is a sifting process, more subject to Providence than to bishops and councils inasmuch as in the far view it looms as a great instance of historical concrescence.

In the light of this process those writings which are approved for the Canon have not simply to be *thought* good enough but to *be* good enough for inclusion. The principle of selectivity is historical in a broader aspect than that of any criteria which the Council might have adopted. The Council of the Canon primarily *recognizes* the worth of these books, it does not constitute this worth even by its important decisions. These decisions are but the final stage of a process that is already fairly mature. Many influential, though unofficial, judgments have already been registered on various portions of Scripture prior to the decisive Synod of Carthage in 397 A.D.

But because a conciliar judgment is essentially an historical judgment (which is not to exclude the activity of the Holy Spirit, but to enhance it), we must admit this theoretically indeterminate boundary of the Canon. One cannot suppose an absolute difference to exist between the *Shepherd of Hermas*, for example, which is said to have been barely kept out, and certain books of the New Testament whose admission was allowed only after debate. The presence of circumstances such as this reveals the absence of any absolute demonstration of limit. So we return to our earlier position with regard to the subject of Inspiration and authority: we have an absolute Revelation, but its absolute character is not to be grasped on its surface—whether in text or canon.

In the most dynamic periods of the Church's history there

has been no major concern for a Canon. In the New Testament age the authority of Scripture depended upon its own spiritual message and force rather than upon any constitution from a source exterior to the word itself. Then, as in the time before, holy men spoke out of their own arresting experience of a "Thus saith the Lord."

The Reformers also could treat the Canon as a very secondary matter. Luther did not hesitate to label one of its New Testament selections as an "epistle of straw" and impugned the judgment which could have admitted it as an inspired writing. And Calvin derided the Roman Church of his day for its arrogance in claiming to be the safeguard of such a canon. He says, "But to submit the sound oracles of God to the Church, that they may obtain a kind of precarious authority among men, is blasphemous impiety." He points out that there is no mention of a Canon in the Council of Nice, and "yet the Holy Fathers then were armed with strong enough weapons against Arius, as they had the Scriptures in their hands." And "secondly," he asks, "what will become of the law and the prophetical books, if their authority continued in suspense till a decision was pronounced two thousand years after the law was given?"[14]

The Bible is now known to have reached its final form only gradually as the dynamic of Christ was transmuted into the Gospels and Epistles of the New Testament. So gradual and natural a thing was the development of this witness that in the case of the Gospels in particular it is doubtful whether it is possible for us to speak of a true "autograph" at all. To do so necessitates the imposition of a definite *moment* upon the formation of the Gospel witness in a way which would be wholly arbitrary and opposed to the nature of the emergence of these records in the early Church.

The appearance of recent new versions and translations of the New Testament has thrown the glare of a spot-light upon one instance of this difficulty. It is the doxology of the

Lord's Prayer, now dropped from the traditional Matthean version of this gem of Christ's teachings. Supposing that this verse of Scripture was added, as the evidence of the manuscripts indicates, half a century later than the time when this Gospel was first cast into something resembling its present form in the Greek—would this fact invalidate the beautiful ascription with which the model prayer closes? No, there are millions of Christians who will insist on following their Lord in saying, "Thine is the kingdom, and the power, and the glory forever," even if in some instances it should mean abandoning the static veneration of an imagined autograph whose aim is an easy objectivity, and whose effect is to put faith in the visible "letter" rather than the invisible God.

The vitality of Scripture offers an occasion not for fear but for encouragement. The finality of the Word of God is not in the form of its human language but in Christ. Was He not in fact, as the philosopher Schelling enquired, the last God?

Whatever of science we may have been able to incorporate in our approach to Scripture, it remains true that our knowledge will amount to little unless completed by faith. By way of philosophy we may strive to make ultimate the coherence of the actual, and this has its value; but as Nels F. S. Ferré points out, we must realize that "faith completes the coherence of truth."[15] Yet, having seen this, we know that the supreme possibility of our faith is still beyond the realm of philosophy. The highest service which philosophy can render is to incline us to submit ourselves personally to Him who alone is equal to the possibilities of faith.

It is not enough that in the language of philosophy we should say of Him that He "receives the past" and "envisages future possibility" as no other instance of world concretion has ever done,[16] or even that we should join the theologian in acknowledging that "He who has risen again is Lord of history, Lord of all times and all dimensions of historical reality in the past, the present, and the future."[17] By faith we must go beyond philosophy and theology to that personal situation in which we can say with the disciple, "My Lord and my God." And this will come to pass only when we have known in our own lives that which Luther recommended for faith in the prescription: "It is that *thou* shouldest hear *thy* God speaking to *thee*."

9

The Church,
the Engaged Community

"... this world that calls itself civilized can be spiritually
healed only if it finds its way back to true Christianity."
—FRANZ WERFEL [*Between Heaven and Earth*, p. 120]

THE unique events of the historic Christ, which were themselves the culmination of the prior messianic development,
left their historical resultant not only in the proclamation of
the New Testament Scriptures, but also in the form of the
Christian Church. No fact of the period following Jesus'
Resurrection is more definite or more primary than the continuity which exists between the Person of Christ and the life
of this institution which issued from His messianic mission
and activity.

This continuity of Christ and the Church appears at many
junctures and under many aspects in the New Testament
account. It is most comprehensively expressed in the doctrine
(for it is much more than a "figure") of St. Paul in which he
speaks of the Church as the "Body" of Christ. This rich and
provocative concept makes it clear that the Church is an
organism, that the life of Christ is really contained within it,
and that it has a peculiar character and function which set
it apart from all other personal associations and groups. As

the vehicle of Christ's real continuity in the historical sphere, it becomes the representative of Christ before the world as well as the agent of His ongoing redemptive purpose. Its individual members are members of the body and their function is to work together in harmonious correlation to serve the purpose of the Head, who is Christ. The Church is the Body, but not in itself the whole Body of Christ. Christ is and remains unmistakably the Head, and the organism is complete only in this relation. It is He who through His Spirit and the abiding revelation that He has made in His Word guides, controls, and sustains the organism.

The history of the early Church reveals that this Body is conscious of being in possession of the unique spiritual power that had belonged to Jesus in the time of His earthly life. The *pneuma* and *dynamis* of this supremely "charismatic" person, the Messiah, have passed over into this corporate group. His gifts and energies are now those of His disciples as they are uniquely banded together in His name. And this is according to the promise that He had made to them that "power" should come upon them. (Acts 1:8)

The Pauline concept of the organic Church is in agreement with what Jesus has given His followers to expect. He had assured them that an inspiring Helper or Supporter would take His place at their side, and that through Him they should do even "greater things" than Jesus has yet accomplished. The spiritual Christ is the vine of which they are branches. Their life is in Him and cannot continue apart from Him.

The Church is the "first fruits" of the whole new order which is being brought in by the Messiah. (I. Cor. 15:23; James 1:18). In this the Church reveals again its close connection with its Lord. Through the Resurrection this new creation proceeds: "Christ the first fruits, afterwards they that are Christ's at his coming." Yet this fruition of the Body is regarded as a fact already existent by virtue of the Church's union with Christ. The Lord was alive in His Church in what was certainly experienced by these early Christians as an *actual* sense. His personality expressed itself and accomplished its designs through this Body. The word "mystical" as applied to this concept of the Body of Christ falls far short of conveying the reality as it was known by them. Thus we do an injustice to this truth when we think of the Church as being Christ's Body in some figurative or symbolic sense alone. The personality of Christ actively overflowed the few years in which He "tabernacled" in the flesh and has continued its historical operation in a fashion that is, to say the least, extraordinary and wholly unparallelled. But it is in a genuinely personal manner that His historic action continues. Only the Body changes as the authentic impulses of the Person of Christ are carried out long after His physical death.

The real organicity of the Church is grounded not only in the experiences in which the Christians knew themselves to be in possession of the Saviour's personal life and potency, but also in certain prior constructs of the peculiar sacramental unity of the Messiah with His elect. Upon this factor as upon many others the eschatological creations of the Inter-Testamental period throw light. The Book of Enoch (especially chap. 39 and following) represents the Son of Man and His righteous ones as being together in heavenly places even before the final judgment occurs. The community of these chosen saints, which from all eternity is bound up with the Christ, is to be made manifest at His coming. The whole process is conceived along distinctly predestinarian lines which appear to be reflected in the views of Paul. Albert Schweitzer, interpreting Paul in the light of this material, writes, "In accordance with this the eschatological concept of the Community of the Elect (that is to say, the predestined solidarity of the elect with one another and with the Messiah) takes on for Paul a quasi-physical character."[1]

This "Community," according to Schweitzer, emerges in the doctrine of Paul as a new order of existence that is precipitated by the messianic dominion of Jesus. Jesus is Himself the first "island-peak" in which the rising order becomes visible.[2] The subsequent portions (the "elect," who are the Church) are thought of as making their appearance in turn, as the process is advanced through further stages implicit in the logic of the eschatological dogma. So Schweitzer traces the idea of the Church as "Body" to this pre-Christian doctrine of a "corporeity" which is the common possession of Christ and His elect.[3] All of which strengthens the impression that the New Testament concept of the Church is one of an actual entity in which the Messiah continues His program of divine action. This inheritance of an almost physical understanding of the Church's nature lent itself, incidentally, to some very costly abuses through which the Church, along with other spiritual entities, was fully hypostatized.

The aspect of this probable connection with the older apocalyptic which is relevant to our present interest is simply that this idea in its primitive stage accentuates the organic concept of the Church which is manifest in the New Testament epistles. It is the Body of Christ in which His people are joined vitally with His own Spirit to perpetuate His individual existence and to advance His mission in the world. As such it has an identity and a real personality that no other society approximates.

The task of the Christian Body is not only to witness to Christ's Messiahship (which is a witness both to the Gospel and to the fact of Judgment); it is also to carry out His will within the fellowship and in relation to life outside this circle. The Church bears the message of Christ; at the same time it is itself the product of His messianic deed, and so, the sphere in which His benefits and graces are already found. The Church is thus both agent and receptacle. It is at once that which is *revealed* and a continuing *revelation* through its faithful exposition of the life which dwells in this Body.

The Church embodies the "mission" of Christ. As He is

sent by the Father to do His will, so He in turn sends His servants to do His will in the world. (St. John 20:21). The Church then, as a whole, is apostolic—not only a living but also a "sent" Body. In that it continues to work the works of Him who has instituted the Church it expands His ministry and, in this active, "opening" sense, even His revelation of Himself. The Church, not officially as if in a narrow and legal administration of its calling, but historically and vitally, is completing the structure of the central biblical experience of Christ as it brings new areas of life under the conscious rulership of His Word and will. The Church is constantly adapting and relating the message of its changeless Gospel to the changing world which is the field of its great commission. This Body, because of its actual continuity with Christ, its possession of the holy mysteries, and its empowerment of God's Spirit, does in a way that is fully pragmatic as well as divinely purposive, hold the "keys to the Kingdom." It "judges the world" also, in the measure in which it sets forth Him in whom all righteousness is consummated, and in answer to whom every man must make his decision. But it is in no humanly conceived "political," church that these powers and privileges consist. It is only to the Church whose completeness and spiritual life are realized in the Headship of Christ that these prerogatives belong. They vanish immediately upon the suggestion that any human vicar of this Head should, by virtue of an institutional position, lay claim to them.

THE CHURCH AND THE SCRIPTURES

A frequent subject of discussion in recent years is the question whether the Church or the Bible has priority in theological importance and authority. There are, even within Protestantism, those who have tended to subtract from the traditional eminence of the Scriptures in this respect in order, as it is supposed, to give larger weight to the doctrine of the Church. Particularly on two scores is it claimed that the authority of the Church overshadows that of the Scriptures.

First it is said, quite broadly, that the Church wrote the New Testament Scriptures. And secondly, it is held that the Church has demonstrated her superiority to the Scriptures in determining the Canon. These assertions, while containing some partial truth, are in the main incorrect and misleading. The issue which they denote is of sufficient theological importance that every well-informed Christian should clarify the matter in his own mind. A presentation of several of the more pertinent aspects of this problem may be helpful toward this end.

The statement that "the Church wrote the Scriptures," is an effective example of abstract, uncautious and non-semantic thinking. The serious inaccuracy of this expression is evident as soon as one has examined the terms involved. There is no realistic definition of the "Church" that can possibly accord with its performing the act of "writing." The Church, as a real whole and as a "Church," cannot write. The nearest actual approach to this notion would be that some individual or company should inscribe, in the name of the Church and as a record of the Church's express mind on certain particular subjects, what the Church through some definitely concerted opinion or conviction had to say. But this, even if it were allowed to be able to justify the claim, is not what appears to have happened. What actually occurred was that *individuals,* within the Church but not *as* the Church, wrote the New Testament books. That is to say, the Scriptures were written by Christian men. These men, it is true, were conditioned by the group (Church) of which they were a part, but it was as spiritually impelled individuals that they wrote. And this is a very different thing from saying that their writing was "individualistic." The orientation of this writing was corporate;

its inspiration and conception were the concrete experience of Christ-filled individuals.

If the writing is to be placed in any other agency than that of these persons (who were many and who built upon the work of one another), the only logical assertion is to say that the Holy Spirit wrote the books through these men. One cannot, with the same degree of accuracy, say that the Church wrote them through these same individuals. For the consciousness of those who wrote was not: "What is the Church directing me to write?"—but rather, "What is the Spirit saying through me to the churches?"

So from the standpoint of linguistic realism it can no more be said that the Church produced the Scriptures than that a certain library produced the book that the author is now engaged in writing. In both cases, the Church and the library are significant and vital factors, but not in the way of explicit agency. Entering into the total situation they exert large and characteristic influence, but not the primary action.

We can say that men wrote the Bible, or that God wrote it (in the less exact sense of "directed and inspired" it) but we cannot with any cogency say that the Church wrote it. It was written *in* the Church, *to* it and *for* it, but not *by* it.

If it is contended that the Church mediated salvation before the New Testament Scriptures came into existence, we should answer that this is literally so, but without much significance in view of the fact that there was operating in this period the pre-literary equivalent of the Scriptures in the oral witness, the *kerygma* of the Apostles. It was still the Word of God, spoken instead of written, that communicated salvation before the New Testament Scriptures; even though it was through the Church, in a general sense, that this Word was transmitted.

On the point of the Church's determination of the Canon, the observations that were made in an earlier section of this study apply here. The Church's function in this regard is not primarily to grant authority to the Scriptures by its decree, though it may conceive of itself as doing just this. What it is mainly doing, in the wider perspective of this decision that it makes, is simply recognizing the authority which these writings have already gathered through their own spiritual worth. The Church can hardly constitute an authority that historical usage has shown to inhere in the superior religious character of the books themselves and so to have been already operative.

The result of this discussion is not to elevate either the Scripture or the Church above the other. The fact is that from the beginning the two factors exert a concomitant witness and effect. The unwritten Word does bring the Church into existence and control its life. This Church, in turn, modifies (in literary and social modes) the dynamic Word in which it is established. The enlarging Word is consonant with a growing Church, as Gospels and pastoral Letters serve to expand the Christian community and are themselves profoundly colored by the developing ecclesiastical experience in which they originate.

The Scripture is superior to the Church in the clarity of its structure and in the normative value which this affords. In its provision of meaning, its insurance of fidelity to the mind of Christ, and its permanent immediacy to the center of the Christian event, the Scripture excels the Church and represents a surer authority. On the other hand, the Church has an advantage over the Scripture in that it is organically related to its Lord in such a manner as to achieve the actual continuity of Christ in time, and to make the living Christ contemporary with every generation of His disciples. The Church is superior, moreover, in the flexibility with which it forms ever new connections between the historic revelation and the challenging present. The Scripture speaks more directly and more unmistakably the mind of Christ, and therefore connotes authority. The Church is the Body of Christ, and as such calls for a reverence in keeping with this exalted definition. The Church and the Scripture are complementary the one to the other. They are not an either-or, but a both-and, proposition; and as such they are together indispensable to the self-disclosure of God as a continuing process.

THE SITUATION AND CHALLENGE OF THE CHURCH TODAY

Through many vicissitudes and changing fortunes the Church has established the amazing record of a fellowship that has endured for nearly two thousand years. In so doing it has exhibited the most striking cultural sequence that history has witnessed; and through every period it has succeeded, in greater or less degree, in being what its Founder intended it to be as His own spiritual agent and organism in the world.

From the historical perspective it is not as alarming as it is from the more restricted viewpoint of the present scene, to have to recognize that the Church has seen more favorable and successful eras. Despite many gains and advantages to which one may point, it is nevertheless true that the Church has a less influential relation to the world's life today than in the periods of its greatest effectiveness. We see in the present a widespread secularization of men's thoughts and attitudes. In many large areas it appears that the world is going about its business without any profound concern for the Christian affirmations and objectives. One could hardly dissent from the forceful diagnosis of A. N. Whitehead who, a few years ago, wrote what is still too obviously true. He said that Protestant Christianity "is showing all the signs of a steady decay. Its dogmas no longer dominate: its divisions no longer interest: its institutions no longer direct the patterns of life."[4]

Clearly the position of the Church in the present time is one that calls for a thorough-going reassessment of its resources and a radical restatement of the truth which it possesses. What is true of lesser organisms would seem to be equally true of the organic Church: if, humanly speaking, it is to survive, it must be able to adapt itself to its shifting environment. It is for the sake of this vital objective that the modern theological synthesis and proposals for cultural reorientation contained in this present work have been set forth. With the conviction that our contemporary religious culture cannot solve its specific and weighty problems by turning back to eminent leaders of former periods as though their situations and their needs encompassed ours, the writer maintains that only a genuinely modern concept of Christian knowledge will meet the actual needs. The impairment of the Church's moral influence, resulting from its obvious forfeiture of cultural control, shows this need of theological adaptation to be urgent.

The primary needs are two: the need for intellectual rehabilitation, and the need for religious and theological unity. And the latter can be effected only as the Church's cultural integrity and relevancy become more apparent.

It must be reiterated that in recent years the most articulate theologies have unfortunately been those that disclaim any significant connections with human culture. The high priest of this varying emphasis is Karl Barth with his ultimatum of a Gospel completely severed from humanistic and scientific knowledge. This mood has alienated those who, in the field of philosophic thought, might have been able to furnish the needed rational cogency to theological ideas. The result is that philosophy rather obtusely dispenses with the central dynamic of Christianity, to the detriment not only of philosophy and theology as cultural sciences, but of civilization itself.

Basic beyond all else is the recognition of the necessity of this intellectual renovation of Christianity in terms of a comprehensive modern view, and a clear indication of the relevance of the biblical facts to the outlook thus achieved. It is tragically erroneous to think that the task of modern Christianity is essentially practical and ecclesiastical, on the supposition that what is needed is only to adjust to our present situation the insights of great Christian thinkers of past ages. If, for example, in order to solve our problems we needed only to bring our churchmanship into accord with the principles of the Reformers, or of Aquinas, or Augustine, a really serious concern for theology could be omitted. But in fact it is not for such an "adjustment" that the present crisis calls. Rather it is a new intellectual enterprise that is demanded.

A PROTESTANT ILLUSION

It seems likely that the most hampering misconception that exists within Evangelical Christianity today is the idea that we need only to go back to the Reformation to solve the problems of contemporary religious culture. This wistful and completely uncritical attitude, which is common to widely differing religious parties, overlooks the seriousness of the historic distance that lies like a chasm between the present epoch and the sixteenth century. It is not simply that the present scene is immeasurably more crucial and threatening. The construction of religious facts and problems is signally different; with the consequence that a totally different address must be made to them. The cultural relativity which this distance of history implies may be evaluated in the following circumstances:

The question at the time of the Reformation was one of securing a better interpretation of Christianity against a worse. Despite the extreme moral and spiritual divergences of this period, the fact remains that the whole gamut of the contest was Christian. Now, on the contrary, the issue is the survival of Christianity itself. The danger then was that the

Church should allow herself to be shameful and corrupt; the danger now is that the Church should allow herself to be ignored and forgotten. Then, the civilization of Europe stood on the threshold of a new age of exhilarating, if thoroughly unsettling, human adventure—the age of Columbus and Copernicus. Today, all civilization totters on the brink of nihilism—in the age of totalitarianism and massive secularism, of the cold war and the atomic bomb.

In the sixteenth century the whole province of culture was within the sphere of the Church, literature and art being mainly subsidiaries of a Christian view of the cosmos. Today, vast new areas of thought demand a consideration as to their place in the theological synthesis. Whereas in the time of Calvin the great body of the humanities offered only variations of the principal religious themes, in the present state of culture the disturbing and unclassifiable voices of Dostoievsky and Nietzsche, Van Gogh and Picasso, Schoenberg and Sartre, are insisting that they be given a hearing of their own. The strange, uncharitable impact of Baudelaire and Rimbaud, of Freud and Kafka, of Joyce and Lawrence, must be evaluated with a totally new candour in the light of the pervasive thought-forms of our age; for these drastic appraisers of the human scene are saying something that we must understand. Most especially, as this study has demonstrated, the powerfully seminal insights of Kierkegaard and Jaspers, of Bergson and Whitehead, are extremely relevant to the reconstruction of the Church's message to man in the modern world. The time has arrived when theology must examine with open mind the thought of men whose conclusions are quite alien to the overt principles of Christianity, for the reason that their bold excavations are often found to illuminate the hidden causes and blindly striving purposes of this period of cultural travail. There is a significant bond of sympathy between these probing intellects and the tragic center of Christianity; and the fact is a hopeful one. For it now ap-

pears that unless we suffer with Christ in an unlimited awareness of life's moral pathos, we shall by no means glory with
Him in a peace which at once embraces and surpasses all
understanding.

Contemporary Christianity must come to realize that the
Reformation may be followed as a dependable guide for
theological rehabilitation, only when it is borne in mind that
this historic movement reveals a radical incompleteness at
two salient points. There are, accordingly, two critical les-
sons of the Reformation which should be heeded by all who
are now seeking an intellectual renaissance within and
around the Christian faith. One of these concerns the organic
failure of the Church in the sixteenth century. And the other
indicates the inadequacy of the religious philosophy to which
the Reformation gave its sanction.

The first of these is the more tangible, namely, the tragedy
that resides in the fact that the protesting elements failed to
achieve on their part, following the revolt from Rome, a convincing unity of the Church. After the Reformation there
continued, in too large a degree of isolation from one another, the giant fragments of the Reformed and Lutheran
Churches on the continent and an equally individual national
church in England. In every quarter there was recognition of
the basic spiritual need for a oneness of the Protestant con-
fessions. And the age is not lacking in dramatic witness to
this need. The overtures of Archbishop Cranmer and of such
continental reformers as Zwingli and Melancthon are representative of the profound concern that arose over this
matter within the first generation of the reform movement.
No more pathetic incident has reached us from the period
of the Reformation than the refusal of the most heroic leader
of the cause in Germany to accept the proffered hand of
Zwingli when, at Marburg, the Swiss reformer had sought
an understanding with the Lutherans across the barriers of
their differing conceptions of the Lord's Supper.

The evangelicals' agreement in protest was never matched by a comparable agreement concerning the articles of faith; and this is especially true at the point of the doctrine of the Church itself. The first and most apparent sign of the incompleteness of the Reformation is this failure of the Protestant element to achieve the full identity that was implicit in its historical mission. To admit that the mission has been only partially successful is to exercise a humility that will in no wise injure the Church's cause.

The other major lesson emerging from a critical study of the Reformation is that this movement was incomplete on the level of its resultant philosophy of religion. Perhaps it could not have been otherwise historically, but now it can be seen that Luther and Calvin, for all their magnificent opposition to the outward and official error of their time, did not proceed to the deepest root of the theological problems which they confronted. They introduced a tremendously vital experience of the Word of God which brought victory in the moment of the Church's crisis, but unfortunately they and their associates left no distinctly Protestant doctrine by way of expressing the relation of this dynamic Word and its authority to the underlying concepts and categories of the prevailing philosophy or to any other system. Consequently, when the historically critical phase of the Reformation had somewhat subsided, the rationale of this mighty movement, its philosophy of religion, was settled tamely upon the age-old prejudice of a scholastic, Aristotelian foundation. So again, as under the Roman Catholic regime, the Church's attempts to speak of the nature of God and of Revelation were cast into the moulds of substantialist, quasi-physical, pre-Christian categories—a course that would greatly impede the future of the Reformation.

It was only because revealed truth could still be thought of as something possessed of a peculiar *quality* (a primary substantialist category) that the "paper pope" of Protestant scholasticism could be enthroned within two generations of Calvin. The limitation of this period, and of centuries to follow, was to consider God, the soul, and divine truth as *things*, comparable to the world of objects. This negative development, so disappointing in comparison with the astounding force of the Reformation's beginning, is to be explained by the fact that the successors of Luther and Calvin devoted themselves to a pious work of refining and explicating their masters' doctrinal points rather than to the more essential task of bearing out the metaphysical implications of the pivotal Reformation truths. The result is that the "Word" of Luther and Calvin suffers, in the final analysis, from the same disability as that of Barth and Brunner: it lacks a deliberate rational connection with the dominant categories of man's response to the world of nature and history. It is true that the teachings of the Reformers generally imply a repudiation of the old philosophical structure, Luther being particularly vehement in this regard, but no theologian of this period undertook the task of proposing a frame of categories to take the place of the reigning Aristotelianism. Thus the reversion to scholasticism was inescapable.

In the genuinely existential situation in which the Reformers first delivered this Word given to them, it needed no philosophical reference whatever. In such a crisis, occurring as it did *within* the Church, the rational content of faith is sensed in the very conditions of the struggle, and these conditions occupy the Christian mind sufficiently. In the historical tension of the Reformation there lay a *direction* which gave promise of new theological meanings, but for which, in the nature of the case, men must wait trustfully. It is this promise and this trust which have lacked fulfillment in the Reformation. When, following the dramatic era, the time was ripe for a constructive metaphysical phase of the Reformation, no action was taken. Consequently, there has been lacking a philosophical differential as between the Protestant and Roman Catholic positions.

As in the early centuries of the Church there had to be formed an intellectual method for the evangelization of Europe (which was very largely effective), and as there did arise at the time of the Reformation the need (largely unsatisfied) for an appropriate Christian philosophy, so in our time there must be such a modern pattern of Christian thought as the writer has indicated. The mind of our age needs to be reached by the Gospel, and culture is the medium of mind. The reconciliation of Christian truth with the most pertinent and convincing of present cultural modes is a towering concern as we endeavor amidst the threats of the current situation to avoid spiritual ruin. When the older categories have long since exhausted their usefulness as vehicles of biblical truth, there is no alternative but to turn to other and more agreeable forms.

THE PRESENT OPPORTUNITY AND ITS PROMISE
FOR THE WORLD CHURCH

In these pages it has been made clear, the writer trusts, that the most far-reaching change that has taken place in the contemporary world of science and philosophy is a vast, yet subtle, emancipation from the totalitarianism of the Greek objectivist categories. For the first time in history new philosophical instruments are available by means of which Christianity may possess a theology that is not alien to its own genius, a new religious metaphysic in which the categories of event, purpose, historic relation and vital process will lend themselves to a new and more effective telling of the supreme story of the meaning of God in history. It is, happily, a philosophical method that is both Christian and contemporary, a manner of thinking which derives its basic ideas not from the visual experience of pre-scientific observation, but from a maturer analytical science, from history (centering in "sacred" history), and from the structure of personal experience as known in its real autonomy and in terms of freedom.

The Church has no sound alternative to this theological transvaluation. The cultural inadequacy of the old is evident. The determination to have no religious philosophy at all serves only to buttress the ailing and unsatisfying world-view to which the hungry minds of men must still indifferently cling. Man will have a theology; the question is whether it will be of any use to his soul, and to his society.

A new theological establishment is particularly essential to the present aspirations of the churches for a more vital and evident unity. It is undoubtedly true that the need of a theology for the Ecumenical Church is immediate. It would be tragic in the extreme if the Christian world should delude itself into thinking that the noble and inspiring organization of the World Council of Churches is equipped already with a theology adequate for the Church's function in the present crisis. Wtihout a more compelling theological position, allied with growing church unity and abetting this unity, there is little hope that Christians will be able to speak the authoritative and redemptive word that our perishing generation wants to hear.

Historically, Protestant Christians have been noted for their readiness to make use of novel viewpoints and modes of understanding as they emerge in reference to anterior and permanent religious truths. It is encumbent upon the free spirit of Evangelicalism to accept the challenge that is indicated now, as the modern synthesis points to an ancient but still continuing Revelation. It may be regarded as certain that Roman Catholic theologians, competent though they are in intellectual adaptation, will be incapable of taking advantage of the new insights so contrary to the static genius of Thomism, a philosophy to which the Roman system would seem to be irrevocably attached. It is therefore a Protestant task, and its vigorous and concerted prosecution will amount to the completion of the Protestant Reformation. Only when this has reached the stage of actual achievement, will there arise the possibility of further and more thrilling adventures in unity.

Not least among the inducements of a renovated theology is the promise which it intimates in reference to the appeal of Christianity to the modern Jewish mind, with its tremendous religious depth, its earnest and inquisitive attitude toward the fact of Christ, and its strong impulse toward a non-substantialist and anti-Hellenic world-view. In its hypostasis of the Godhead traditional Christian doctrine has maintained an infraction against the faith of Israel which, perhaps more than any other factor, has precluded its corporate acceptance of the historic Christ. The offense has been far greater than the essential Christian idea would have necessitated. Recent events make it appear quite conceivable that even yet the Protestant and Jewish faiths may be joined before the Christian fold is itself entirely set in order through a reconciliation with the Church of Rome. If this does amazingly occur, may the Christian world have grace enough to regard the religious act of Israel as the true *reversion* that it is, instead of the *con*version which it is only in minor part. Our prayer that "Israel might be saved" should be offered in this spirit alone. But it should be offered fervently; and all the more so now, because the theology of the cultural synthesis is much closer to the patterns of Hebraic thought than is the older style of a late-Hellenic world-view.

Before the Church can have re-union, it must have re-birth. And it is not arrogance to observe that Christian rebirth at this level can take place only on condition of the intellectual renewal of which we have spoken. This is the role of a religious philosophy that is at once fully modern in its scientific spirit, and originally and powerfully Scriptural in its message and underlying thought-form.

There is every reason to believe that such a philosophy will not only bridge the lamented gap between science and faith but also prepare the way doctrinally for the "Coming Greater Church" which is the desire of so many Christians in this age of disunity and disheartening moral impotence. It is a consummation devoutly to be wished, and it is a task that cannot be postponed.

The Church in our time must be a Church Cognizant if it hopes to be a Church Triumphant.

10

Salvation: Experience and Expectation

"Everyone who recognizes a meaning of history, recognizes salvation through history, for without salvation history would fall into the abyss of a demonic meaninglessness."
—PAUL TILLICH [*The Interpretation Of History*, p. 283]

CHRIST is the bearer of world meaning, and history is the history of salvation. The two propositions are closely related in that meaning is a vital aspect of salvation, and the historic Christ is both the original and the abiding means by which salvation is realized. In Him the whole sequence of God's saving activity in history has its meaningful center.

Within its rich variety the biblical idea of salvation manifests a unity which is that of the history itself. The form in which the history is initiated is a national experience of salvation which influences the idea through its entire course until its fulfillment in the Gospel of the New Testament. The changing fortunes of this idea, with the corresponding experiences of those whose life depended upon its integrity, tell the story of its gradual refinement and its eventual completion in Jesus Christ.

Salvation means God's provision for the need of His people in whatever situation this need is felt. It is safety, soundness,

176

basic well-being, at many junctures and in many forms. As
Paul S. Minear has expressed it,

> The content of the message of salvation was thoroughly con-
> ditioned by the situation to which it was addressed. Its sanc-
> tion-quotient was affected by current scales of value, by the
> prevailing fears and hopes, by what was considered neces-
> sary to the abundant life.[1]

In the earlier periods of Old Testament history this experience was one of divine guidance and protection in Israel's
political existence. Deliverance from the Egyptian bondage
and the entrance into the land of promise were events whose
memory would for centuries evoke the deep consciousness
of God's salvation. For it was through these that God has
made known His ways unto Moses and His mighty acts unto
the children of Israel.

There are two distinct strains of the doctrine of salvation
within the Old Testament. One is the prophetic and the other
is the sacrificial. According to the latter, God's favor is to
be secured through a ceremonial system which expresses
man's dependence upon God and his readiness to obey Him.
But the sacrificial sin offering goes further than recognition
and worship. At least the beginnings of a theory of moral
justice are seen in those animal sacrifices in which the offering is thought of as taking the place of the sinner and suffering death in his stead. The vivid instance of the scape-goat
(Lev. 16) is a variation of this sacrificial conception.

The prophetic view puts no confidence in this method of
securing God's help through sacrifice. Certainly it cannot
regard the sacrifice as efficacious in itself. Amos, for example,
declares that God despises feasts and burnt offerings, and
that what He really desires from His worshippers is justice.
What God will "not despise," affirms the Psalmist, is "a
broken and contrite heart." The God who was faithful to His

elect ones in the time of the Exodus, who delivers them from recurrent dangers, gives them victory over their enemies, and general prosperity and strength, is not satisfied with anything less than a moral fidelity to His Covenant.

In the Psalms and in the "prophets of individualism," Jeremiah and Ezekiel, this spiritual conception of man's response to God becomes a doctrine of personal salvation from sin. It is the creation of the "new heart" and it revolves around the specifically moral ideas of loyalty and apostasy, repentance and forgiveness. As a theology of the individual's relation to God this emphasis of the later prophets tends clearly toward a doctrine of the future life.

SALVATION IN THE NEW TESTAMENT

The paramount theme of Jesus is the Kingdom of God. His teaching with regard to salvation, whether by word or example, is in reference to this concept. The connections, however, are not always immediately evident. For notwithstanding this kingdom evaluation, there is a constant human factor in His redemptive concern that gives an undiluted concreteness and naturalness to all that He reveals in this central aspect of His ministry. If salvation is for the Kingdom, it is at the same time for a fullness of life in the here and now. The human as well as the divine objective is served on every occasion in which Jesus applies the idea of salvation. The occasions are remarkably varied and they are as fully personal as the individuals to whom He ministered. To be saved is to enter the Kingdom of God. It is also to become the right kind of person and to enjoy the best kind of life.

If there is one saying of Jesus that is representative of the saving transformation that He brings into human life, it is His oft-repeated words, "Thy faith hath made thee whole." To the woman who has touched the hem of His garment He confides, "Daughter, be of good comfort, thy faith hath made thee whole." (Matt. 9:22). For a blind man who has believed in Him He has a similar, "Go thy way; thy faith hath made thee whole." (Mark 10:52). To a grateful leper who has been healed by Him Jesus speaks the same words (Luke 17:19). And to the ruler of the synagogue whose daughter has just died He gives the amazing word, "Fear not: believe only, and she shall be made whole." (Luke 8:50). The word that occurs in each of these instances is a form of the verb *sōzō*, which is "to save" or "to make sound." Thus it appears on these numerous occasions that the salvation recorded is the *making whole* of a life that in one way or another is broken or defeated, sick or lost.

A kindred adjective that Jesus uses is one that brings the thought still closer to that of *health*. It is *hygiēs*, which means sound, wholesome, or whole. He addresses a lame man in John 5:6, "Wilt thou be made whole?" The word is that from which our *hygiene* is derived. The want of wholeness may be physical or spiritual or both. The same Christ who says, "Thy sins be forgiven thee," can also say, "Pick up thy bed and walk." Cases in which the want of wholeness is religious are quite as much in evidence as those in which the illness is bodily. According to the particular fracture from which the personality is suffering Jesus provides the cure, whether it be for a Nicodemus or a Zacchaeus, a Samaritan woman or a dying thief.

Into the wholeness which characterizes salvation other ideas enter to compose and qualify this general designation. These facets of salvation are brought out impressively in the Gospel narrative. One of them is sonship to God as Father. (Matt. 5:45). And closely linked with this is *likeness* to the Father. Another is the return to true selfhood, as when the Gadarene maniac is "in his right mind," and the Prodigal Son comes "to himself." Man is so constituted by His Creator that he comes to himself only as he comes to God.

A very large group of salvation motifs is that which surrounds the idea of *rest*, as deliverance from anxiety and fear. Nowhere is the real humanness of Jesus' redemptive mission so apparent as here. Only the experience of *forgiveness* occupies a place of comparable importance, and it is really inseparable from what He has to say of rest and peace.

"Come unto me, all ye that labour and are heavy laden, and I will give you rest." This soul-refreshing word of Jesus, when rightly understood, is as soteriological as any invitation, pronouncement, or promise that Jesus ever made. To secure His *rest* is in every way, experiential and present as well as theological and final, to be saved. He saves men from the fear that both paralyzes and consumes. He delivers from anxiety. The word *anxious* does not appear in the Authorized Version of the New Testament, but the Revised Standard Version (following Weymouth, and Torrey) uses this more sensitive word in place of "Take no thought for your life . . ." (Matt. 6:25)[2] It makes extremely meaningful to our own time this blessed injunction in which Christ speaks to a need that has altered little since the day of His Sermon on the Mount. "Be not anxious" is the message of this singular appeal as best interpreted for the present. It is *"Sorget nicht,"*[3] to an age that, in the description of Martin Heidegger, is the age of *care (Sorge).*

"Come unto me, all ye that labour . . ." The word that we read as "labour" means exhausted with wearisome effort. The French Bible puts it literally, *fatigués.* It is to the one who is "worn out," the utterly weary in spirit, that the redemptive word of Jesus comes with its offer of rest.

Last of all—not that it should seem less important, but that it should carry the full weight and accumulated concreteness of all the foregoing—is the fact that Christ saves men from sin. With all other ills it has its intimate connection. Of the whole burden of man's finitude it is the most unmistakable sign. It is the most injurious of all violations of that wholeness in which a man's life should consist. For sin is the willful separation of the soul from God. It is a double infirmity because it is a voluntary one.

Sin is self-seeking and self-adulation. It is unloving and pride and numerous other perversions of the God-given impulse of man's life. But it is basically a wrong relation to God. It is denial where there should be recognition, ingratitude in place of love, distance preventing communion, death usurping life. This vitiated reference of man's spiritual being is not something apart from his anxiety, and from the illness and fragmentariness of his being. Fear is unbelief, care is something other than the trust which is born of love. Desperation is far from reverence. From the sin which is both brokenness and guilt Jesus, by His word and by His fulfilling and atoning death, by a perfect love which casts out fear, saves as He forgives the sinner.

All this and much more besides, is the human content which Jesus pours into the generic term *salvation*. From the Godward and objective angle it is His seeking and saving that which is *lost*. Any need of salvation is a being lost and a waiting for divine discovery. In the same historical and objective sense His gift of salvation is, by His own definition, a "ransom for many." When Jesus restores the life that is misplaced, mends that which is broken, forgives the guilty, and turns alienation and revolt into love and service, He is effecting the atonement of man with God. The thoroughness and scale of His redemptive action are such that His most able interpreter could reach no other conclusion than that "God was in Christ, reconciling the world unto Himself."

In the Gospel of John the meaning of Christ's saving ministry is told in such a way as to place the emphasis upon the *person* of Christ and the fellowship which the disciple has with Him through believing. The eschatological horizon of the other Gospels recedes and the message of salvation is to a large extent "interiorized," and at the same time universalized beyond the peculiarly biblical scheme of an imminent and literal terminus of history. Decision and judgment are still prominent, as they must be in any true reaction to Christ's Gospel, but the focus is now upon the religious experience in which one is united with Him who is the Lord of life—an uninterrupted life embracing time and eternity. Salvation, in John, is the personal knowledge of God through Christ; and whoever has entered upon this vital relationship *has* eternal life now. The meaning of the messianic future is concentrated in the believer's present experience. For him who is a true branch of this life-giving vine the Kingdom of God has already come. Those who are "given" to Christ are in "the world," but they are not "of the world." Through the Father's name they are "kept" from the evil, in victorious oneness with the Son and the Father.

If Jesus' pronouncement of salvation is "Thy faith hath made thee whole," the characteristic and confident inference of Paul is, ". . . we have peace with God through our Lord Jesus Christ." His interpretation is founded mainly upon the idea of God's moral government. Yet his *legal* viewpoint is revolutionary and is attended with the profoundest contributions to the historical and psychological understanding of Christian truth. While the center is a legal conception of God's righteousness, the range of this interpretation of the Gospel is broad enough to include every phase of human concern, and the net result is history's most powerful denial of legalism.

We have peace with God through our Lord Jesus Christ because we are "justified by faith." (Romans 5:1) In the *fact* of justification Paul's doctrine stands fully within the legal system. In the *means* of justification his teaching is a clear enunciation of a grace of God which, by a peculiar paradox of the Gospel, both vindicates the legal idea and forever undoes it by retiring it to a secondary place in the divine economy. Love supplants the law in the great theological gospel of St. Paul in a manner which affords the supreme explanation of the place which Christ's redemption has in the over-all view of Scripture. Paul's account of Christ in Romans is the most profound of the Bible's great intimations of the philosophy of history.

The apostle follows Christ in asserting that His death was an offering for our sin. "Christ died for us," (Romans 5:8), is the classic and absolute summary of the Gospel message. There is no mistaking that His death is for "the ungodly," (5:6) and that it is in the nature of a "propitiation" for the "remission of sins." (3:25) But that it is nothing more than a propitiation and that its meaning does not reach beyond the sacrificial and the legal, Paul certainly does not suggest. On the contrary he shows that it touches and transforms every sphere of life. Not only is it "justification and reconciliation." Being redeemed by Christ is to be "re-created," "reborn," "adopted" as a child into the family, "translated" into a new mode of existence, and above all, to be "in Christ."

Salvation, according to Paul, does indeed look toward the future and final event of eschatology, but at the same time it has also a present reality. What the Christian already knows of the grace of Christ is the "earnest" of the perfected future. The apostle knows whom he has believed and is fully persuaded as to the surety of the commitment that he has made in Christ. It is as certain as if that "Day" had arrived. Four splendid freedoms has Christ brought in His salvation. He has (1) taken away the *wrath* of God, and freed us from (2) sin, (3) the law, and (4) death.[4] The issue of all this is "peace with God through our Lord Jesus Christ."

It is doubtful whether many Christians realize and accept for their own spiritual outlook the thoroughness with which Paul makes grace to "abound" over wrath and law, as well as over sin and death. What really occurs here is that the law (the religious command, pressure of conscience, duty) is made to abdicate its rule of the Christian's life. The law is no longer our master, for we have a new preceptor in the gracious and constraining spirit of Christ. Paul clearly maintains that it shall henceforth be the law of love or nothing. The law of command has failed, and its failure could hardly be given a more final and unqualified description than that which Paul has given it. The law was preparatory and it has served its time. It has revealed to man not his righteousness but his universal inability to be righteous on the basis of moral effort. The law has only manifested man's spiritual need. And when this need has appeared, it is seen to be a need of that which must transcend the law.

In the light of the revelation of God's grace in Christ, he who has made his "boast of the law" will make it no more. (Romans 2:23). The commandment "which was ordained to life," the apostle has found in his own experience "to be unto death." (7:10). Though the law has served God's purpose in making sin known and grace appreciated, it has in itself contributed only to man's shame and defeat. For sin has taken "occasion by the commandment" to work in the human heart "all manner of concupiscence." (7:8) The law has in fact caused sin to flourish, and has necessitated some other solution to the moral problem. Hence in the fullness of the times God sent forth His Son to "redeem them that were under the law." (Galatians 4:4) God has redeemed from sin *and* from the law!

Because God has so acted, the Christian is like a widow who is free to marry again. The law being not only demoted but "dead" and gone, the believer ought now to join himself to another, even "him who is raised from the dead, that we should bring forth fruit unto God." (Romans 7)

This displacement of the moral command as the motivation of Christian action is the keystone both of Paul's psychology and of its dogmatic expression. But, as the writer has already intimated, there are seemingly very few who are ready to follow the apostle in this startling doctrine, and most of us are still trying to achieve righteousness by forcing ourselves to be "good" on the basis of a moral command. Consequently, our religious principles and our natural emotions are often in terrific opposition to each other, and the "wrath of God," though in a diminishing and duller sense, is still the portion of many. When the law's requirement is distasteful and virtue is the outcome of strenuous endeavor, our righteousness will be meager and our guilt inescapable.

We will not trust ourselves with a doctrine of grace, though we have every inducement to do so. In the essential structure of our moral impulses most of us are still on the other side of the Damascus Road. That "all have sinned and come short" is not difficult to grasp, but the "free gift" of righteousness is too little appropriated and its "peace" too seldom evident. Grace remains incredible and the law still dominates unfaith. It could be otherwise, if we would really forego the independence of our moral ambitions and the fearful compulsion of the "wrath of God."

In the early church salvation was both eschatological event and present experience. The two aspects are complementary and are remarkably balanced in the New Testament materials on this theme. This fact is shown in a tabulation which H. Wheeler Robinson has made of the instances of the terms "salvation" and "save" in the whole of the New Testament. He has found that there are one hundred and fifty-one instances of the Greek equivalents of these words, of which more than two-thirds are in the verb form as distinguished from the noun. This indicates that the active conception of salvation is more prominent in the Scriptures than the representation of it as a condition or a state. But this is, at the moment, incidental. What bears upon our present subject is that there are thirty-three instances in which salvation refers to "the experiential content of the deliverance (faith and conduct)," and exactly the same number of instances which Robinson regards as "the eschatological completion of the deliverance." The other references are to deliverance from disease, demon-possession, physical death, and more general types. From this variety and equilibrium of emphasis on the *here* and the *hereafter*, Robinson draws the conclusion that salvation meant "deliverance from any kind of ill, and the specific faith of the Christian increased the intensity, without limiting the extensity, of the general experience of being 'saved,' by whatever means."[5]

Since New Testament times the doctrine of salvation has attached itself mainly to the distinctly "spiritual" pattern of religious conversion. It has tended to formalize this experience and has often lost sight of its wider implications and accomplishments. Yet in this very emphasis it has kept clear and foremost what is in fact most central in the Christian experience of salvation. The successive periods of church history present, for the most part, changing emphases upon the various aspects of this characteristic experience. In the time of the Reformation, for example, the question that preoccupies the Christian mind is: what must we do in order to be justified before God? How may we attain to peace of soul and have the assurance of pardon and of life eternal? It is a time, accordingly, when the doctrine of justification by faith comes into great prominence. Other periods have stressed "sanctification," Christian vocation, and the warmth of evangelical experience. In our own time the doctrine of salvation has become broader, both in its view of personality and in its concern with social factors.

THE ESSENTIALS OF SALVATION AND THEIR RELEVANCE
TO CONTEMPORARY NEEDS

In the various concepts which we have been considering there are certain constant factors which determine the character of biblical salvation. First, it is always God, and not someone or something else, who accomplishes salvation. To be "saved" is to know that in some particular way one has been the recipient of God's action. As one writer has expressed it, "No Christian has ever reported his conversion without a *theo-centric* interpretation. It was *God* who did it all."[6] While there is a subjective response, the operation is objective and is God's.

As God is the only source of salvation, so the ground of salvation is always *grace*. What He alone can do for man, He does freely. Inasmuch as through Christ He does for us what we cannot do for ourselves and yet ought to do by virtue of our debt to God, salvation in its fullness is vicarious. The substitutionary idea emerges clearly in the history of Christ, both in the messianic preparation and in the New Testament interpretation of His death. That He was "made sin for us" is a conviction that the first Christians derived from the Savior Himself.

Salvation entails the knowledge of God. We do not receive His gift without knowing something of His attitude and nature. In some measure this knowledge is the prerequisite of redemption; to a much larger extent it is the consequence of the saving experience. To receive His grace is to know Him personally. For this reason redemption and revelation are often embraced in one theological item. Salvation is an experimental knowledge of God. Because this knowledge is involved and particularly because God's act in salvation brings to the individual a fuller understanding both of himself and of his relation to God as a part of a larger redemptive plan, salvation is always in some degree a triumph of *meaning*. And this thought connects immediately with what we have found to be so conspicuous in Jesus' own concept of salvation, namely, the fact of *wholeness*.

He who gives wholeness to Israel and to the world-process bestows it also upon the individual person. Wholeness, with

Jesus, is unquestionably, the badge of holiness. Constant in the salvation which Jesus provides is the thought of being made whole through faith. This experience is a change by which a person is made right with God and within himself. The "wholesome" altering of this basic, though intangible, relation is the means of establishing satisfying relations in respect of all else. Minear has put this thought incisively by saying that, "God is the 'middle term' in every earthly affiliation."[7]

No single aspect of salvation is more relevant to human need in the present than the *wholeness* which the term originally connotes. Certainly no form of salvation could be more applicable to the contemporary situation than one which promises meaning.

The cultural and religious chaos of our modern world exhibits two principal aspects: a *mental* one whose feature is dislocation and unmeaning, and its *emotional* counterpart which is anxiety and fear. An impression that world-experience has no integrity and makes no sense results naturally in a feeling of insecurity and tragic frustration. It is the testimony of more than one practicing psychologist that they have never been able to straighten out and rehabilitate the crippled personalities of those who do not believe in God. Mental health can be achieved only where there is, in the personal situation and the "universe" which it envisions, the sense of wholeness which the name of health invokes.[8]

The anxiety which spreads from the absence of meaning is no small part of the psychic unrest which is now prevalent. While this is, of course, far from being the only source of tension, it is the most pervasive and ruinous in the twentieth century. The disintegration of the mental supports of our specific cultural and religious evaluations has imparted a unique and indelible color to the dominant psychological term of our age, *anxiety*.

Anxiety is variously defined, according to the background and aim of those who study it. The "depth" psychologists describe it in terms of their particular understanding of the psyche and its unconscious drives. Theologians derive it from the dialectical stricture of a life that has both finite and transcendent compulsions, as of a "citizen of two worlds." The emotional fear and tension are common to all viewpoints.

The psychologists are impressively concrete in their accounts of the way in which anxiety fastens itself upon the ordinary facts of personality and bends them continually toward the neurotic. Alfred Adler, who was one of the original "big three" of analytical psychology, saw anxiety as the product of the individual's failure to measure up to the "guiding fiction," or "symbolic style," which he has set for his life. The goal of one's behavior is an "Ego-ideal" which expresses the will to power. Adler says that the formula, "I wish to be a complete man" is the guiding fiction in every neurosis,[9] and that "the ideal of personal importance" is a "point toward which all efforts are directed," molding the mentality, traits of character and predispositions of the neurotic personality in its own image.[10] This over-tense personal ideal acquires in some instances an absolute rigidity, "which assumes nearly an identity with God . . ."[11] This, as anyone can recognize, is the origin of anxiety in the fact of chronic selfishness.

Karen Horney, a noted contemporary psychoanalyst, believes that anxiety rises from one's feeling that he is "little," "helpless," "isolated," and "alone" in the world. Anxiety differs from fear in that the latter is roughly proportionate to the known danger which one has to face, whereas "anxiety is a disproportionate reaction to danger, or even a reaction to imaginary danger."[12] More vague than fear, anxiety is an experience only partially realized. Dr. Horney has an illuminating statement with regard to the ways in which people seek relief of this tension. She writes: "In our culture there are four main ways of escaping anxiety: rationalize it, deny it, narcotize it; avoid thoughts, feelings, impulses and situations which might arouse it."[13] The most significant thing about this statement, from the Christian standpoint, is that this keen and influential spokesman for psychology does not clearly indicate that a religious solution is even attempted, though she may be including it in one or more of the four patterns which she mentions. But it is plain enough that the human predicament which she so ably describes in her books is a plea for that which, in the simpler terminology of religion, is personal salvation. The four solutions which she cites would seem to be inadequate.

A contemporary and promising movement in the area of psychological analysis is that developed by Ludwig Binswanger, Eugene Minkowski and other philosophical European experimenters, known as "existential analysis," or *Daseinsanalyse*. This combines elements of the Freudian technique with the existential view of psychic experience. Thus the practitioners of this type of analysis put great stress upon the frustration and "existential vacuum" which they find to be the most prominent symptoms of many of their patients. Such a condition reflects immediately the mood of the present time, of which alienation, ambiguity, and futility are dominant features.

It is to this situation that the message of salvation in our time must speak, and speak unequivocally, if it is to match the breadth and seriousness of the present need. And to this situation it can speak effectively when the meaning of the Bible's unique event is grasped in its relation to personal reality as interpreted in the historical and organic mode of modern thought.

THE PRESENT CONTENT OF SALVATION

Both to the mental and to the emotional pole of the current dilemma, the biblical message directly applies. In the former respect it is through its revelation of world-meaning that it meets this cultural-religious need. Salvation, in its broadest present-day potential, is just this: that one should see the wholeness of historical occurrence, including its redemptive relevance to the present scene. On the intellectual side and in the extremity of our cultural confusion, salvation is *meaning*. The Gospel, as the vital word in which the messianic interpretation of history culminates, has the only final answer to the problem of a formless existence.

On the side of the emotional consequences of the ambiguity and vacuousness of modern life—in respect of fear, anxiety and guilt—the Christian Gospel has a therapy which is sufficient even for this intractable and overwhelming type of illness. This therapy is the thorough-going contact of the wounded individual ego with the healing Christ. It is a contact which, psychologically, is identification and "transference." In its existential aspect it is encounter and communion, the knowledge of a Person who transcends personality even as He completes it.

It is not a theoretical, but an actual, experiential removal of guilt that occurs in this wholly personal relation to the suffering and reconciling Redeemer. Through identification with Christ the "patient" (the spiritually ill individual who is the minor "sufferer" in this relation) receives forgiveness and also a likeness to the character of the One with whom the identification is made. Some hint as to how this is effected and what its specific issues are, is given in this psychological interpretation of R. S. Lee:

> Identification with him is encouraged first by the way he identified himself with man and secondly by the fact that he suffered the very penalties that we, in our unconscious, fear as the just punishment of our unconscious crimes, whose derivatives we openly confess. He is our representative, the perfect man accepting that punishment on our behalf, though as an individual he did not merit it.[14]

This allusion to the "unconscious" is significant. It indicates that the Christian therapeutic is able to go beneath that guilt of which the patient is aware, to the deeper intrapsychic sources of tension. There is that in the absolute pathos of the cross which plumbs the farthest depths of the soul's most primal structure. The uncharted mechanisms of the origin of anxiety and guilt are spiritually adjusted by the unique datum of the perfect righteousness-in-love of Christ.

The Christ with whom we identify ourself leaves His mark upon us. That which takes place in ordinary instances of identification is here much more pronounced and, because of the moral singularity of Christ's Person, is in the form of a "saving" experience. My being "in Christ" by way of this psychological and religious union, becomes naturally "Christ in me." It is the one example of transference[15] in which this mechanism may be allowed full course without any peril whatever to the individual who is thus yielding himself to the Person of Christ. The only possible risk is that the identification involved should fall short because of a misunderstanding of Christ's real character, and thus yield a commitment that is less than Christian. Only a properly guided Christian education can insure the fidelity of the idea of Christ with which the religious individual begins. The Bible is the truest criterion.

It is of paramount importance that one should note this difference between an authentic and a distorted identification. The author of *Freud And Christianity* makes a penetrating and valuable contribution to the understanding of salvation at this point. He shows that there is a fatal distinction between being "filled with Christ" and being "obsessed with him." The Christ-filled character is one who has identified himself with the real Christ, the life-affirming Lord of love, and who has thus really grown to be like Him. This identifying Ego has, as Lee puts it, "gained a new outlook, freed from the domination of the Super-ego, which manifests itself by a frenzied insistence on the destructive, vengeful wrath of God."[16]

This conception of a Super-ego religion with its permanent obsession with sin, guilt and punishment, is the opposite of the desirable Ego type in which the emphasis is on love, integrity, and freedom. Through Christ the personality achieves the needed balance of the tensions which exist between the Id (instinctual drives), the Super-ego (moral censor) and the moderating Ego.

Unlike the savage and tyrannical Super-ego, the Ego-religion of Jesus grasps the real world and gives effective expression to the impulses coming from the Id. Thus it resolves conflict, achieves psychological normality, and opens the way to the abundant life that God wills for His children. God is no longer the projection of, or the substitute for, the Super-ego, but the living God revealed in the completely harmonious personality of Jesus. To know Him is "life" in a very real and ultimate sense.

The correspondences between this psychological concept of salvation and the particular expression of Christian experience that we have seen in Paul are very suggestive. In both interpretations there is a deliberate reduction of the idea of the "wrath" of God as an enduring and primary constituent of the religious consciousness. In both views the whip-lash conception of an absolutely moral control is displaced by the factor of divine grace. The principle of ethical guidance (Super-ego, and revelation of righteous will) is not discarded. There is still a place for a Super-ego whose powers are appropriately restricted. The moral ideal continues to function but in subordination to the more effective motives of grace. As Kierkegaard says in his *Training for Christianity*, the "Thou shalt" of the law becomes a "future" rather than a "command" to the one who loves God. The true disciple does not have to be forced to do that which above all his heart desires.

It has become fairly evident that the moral absolute is no longer to be regarded as the central Christian reality. Nor does the sovereignty of God depend upon this deification of the punitive idea. And as for salvation, it can very nearly be defined in terms of man's release from this type of spiritual bondage. A practicing psychologist who indicates a definitely Christian allegiance makes a statement which illustrates (in a manner which apart from this context would appear extreme) the soreness of this problem. It is David Seabury who writes, "From experience in psychological work, if I were asked what one factor causes most of our suffering, I would certainly say the delusion of duty. Nothing else causes so much neurosis, insanity and disease. It is the curse of curses."[17]

This malady which roots in the distortion of the moral principle can be cured only through the appropriation of the "higher righteousness" of Christ. Duty will be reinstated only in the grace which can empower it with spiritual desire. Obligation, abstracted from the law of love, is but affliction; and the realization of this fact is essential to any effective renovation of the moral idea.

To the spiritual need of our time the living Christ is in literal fact the supreme physician. There is that in the success of His own personal being, His divine connection and His human understanding, which fits Him completely for this modern ministry. Karl Menninger says, "For all phychotherapy depends for its effectiveness on the extent to which the physician is able to give the patient something he needs and cannot get or cannot accept—love."[18] There could not be a clearer call for the help of the Christ who answers this description in the Gospels and in the continuing experience of those who know Him. As Menninger goes on to recognize, no human being is "great enough, constant enough, omnipotent enough or ubiquitous enough to supply all the love that such individuals need,"[19] and it is for this reason that religion, with its positive resources of faith and love, furnishes an incalculable therapeutic benefit to millions. If in this sense it is true that religion has been the world's psychiatrist throughout the centuries, it is especially true of the Christ who makes men whole. Jesus stands for life, and the religion of Jesus is a life-affirming faith. In this religion alone righteousness and love secure their perfect meeting .

Our basic need is for an understanding of Christian love. Of all religious principles it has tended to be the most nebulous—and this in spite of the concreteness of the cross and the astonishing integrity of the life of Jesus. A primary challenge to religious philosophy today is to interpret this principle in terms that extend beyond the familiar "*eros* versus *agapé*" of religious psychology. Love's real dynamic and its function in the achievement of historical and personal wholeness must be better understood. Not the love of intellect but the intellectualization of love is the form of this theological task.

THE CHRISTIAN EXPERIENCE OF SALVATION

The crisis of the historical process is duplicated in the conversion experience of the individual. As the divine movement in history is completed and its integrity vindicated only through its arrival at an absolute impasse, so the individual personality is established through the humiliation of an unmitigated consciousness of moral want. Salvation, on the human and historical side, is by virtue of the "absurd" factor of moral impossibility.

The "poor in spirit" are none other than those who, in a failure that leaves no historical possibility, have fully realized this moral incompetence. They have come to know, with St. Paul, that it shall not be "by works." It is only when the individual is ready to renounce his "righteousness" as well as his sin, that the healing reversal takes place. The tension of the self-centered life in many instances finds its last stronghold in the determined righteousness of private moral effort. It is the rejection of this that, more than any repudiation of "pleasure" and of "worldliness," constitutes the spiritual revolution. For it is in the moral collapse that the transition from "law" to "grace" occurs in the spiritual crisis. The gift of the Gospel is to "sinners," whose only relation to righteousness is a desperate "hunger and thirst." When the soul has descended to the lowest depths of disgrace, fear and longing, it is surprised to find only God there. In an uncalculated instant God's peace supplants man's pain. In this critical moment of absolute degradation the infinite sufferer, if one is so blessed as to have heard of Him, speaks comfort to the broken and contrite heart. The signal for His entrance is the crucial instant in which the tension of the self-oriented existence becomes so unbearable that the individual has no alternative but to renounce it. This is the psychological content of

> Nothing in my hands I bring,
> Simply to the Cross I cling.

Personal identification with the suffering of Christ brings invariably a consciousness of the vicarious role which inheres in His unreasonable and unseemly pain. It is as evident that He does not deserve the penal stroke, as it is that I do deserve it. I can only conclude that He bears the punishment for me. I can feel, moreover, that by "His stripes" I am in my own being healed and renewed. A sense of pardon and a consciousness of what is most certainly "peace" possesses my being.

In this radical alteration of one's moral being, it is impossible to say exactly what does take place. There is no doubt a profound re-organization and a drastic re-orientation of all the psychic values. Norburg suggests the nature of this spiritual event by saying:

As an existential totality-experience it takes in fear, resistance, self-pity, self-hatred, heroic courage, despondent hopelessness, guilt and emptiness, contradiction and persuasion; then a daring leap—and no one will ever be able to tell whether it was the coward or the courageous one who leaped. *The whole chaos leaped.*[20]

One thing is clear; in this existential encounter of the soul with Christ there is that which effectively banishes the autonomy of the self. The human ego no longer tries to be the center of its universe. It looks with gratitude and trust to its emancipator, and with humble and affectionate concern on other souls. Freed from nervous combativeness it is now a tower of strength to those who need love. It has in fact learned to love God with the whole of life and to love one's neighbor as oneself.

Participation in the existential crisis of the Savior is catharsis, in part. But it is more. It is dedication and it is life. As an existential choice, it is not a willful determination to achieve certain moral objectives; it is rather the willing acceptance of what the crisis revelation presents. It is satisfaction with, and acquiesence in, the will of God. It is the reconciliation of the individual with his spiritual destiny.

The concept of the new divine order and the new being which we find in the profoundest Kingdom-doctrines of the New Testament encourage us to adopt the view that salvation is in large part the attainment of true being. The individual soul, in this view, is to be thought of as the divinely created *possibility* of being. The person is principally a "rôle," as the Latin term suggests, which may be fulfilled or forfeited, as the individual stands before God and answers Him. One realizes *being* through one's decision for Christ. One does not decide for the ultimate as such, but for the Christ who is the ultimate. The most truly existential is the most personal.

To be lost is for the soul to waste away into non-being, through the evasion of its God-given rôle. To be saved is to reach authentic selfhood in response to the pioneer of real identity. "If any man be in Christ he is a new creation."

Salvation is a house of many mansions. Its bearing upon our present situation and its offer to our present need are as full and as relevant and challenging as the Christian message can possibly have been in the first century. The Christ who is as near now as ever, who is quite abreast of our latest psychology and fully cognizant of our particular neuroses and peculiarly modern tribulations, is today more than ever saying, "Be not anxious . . . Come unto me, all ye that labour and are heavy laden and I will give you rest." Salvation is constant and the saving Christ is not obsolete. If we are but willing, we may still receive the gracious dismissal, "Thy faith hath made thee whole."

This Christ is not estranged from the modern scene. Across every barrier, whether of ancient eschatology or of elite modern dogma, He speaks directly to us. From the end to the beginning He knows us as one who is fully contemporary with us. He is as close to the natural as to the holy mysteries. He does not frown upon life but only upon its desecration. In His confession there is no good thing that is not allowable to them that love God. He is the inspiration of all who have dared to say, "Love God and do as you please." There is no condemnation to them that are in Christ Jesus. He came not for judgment but for abundant life. Not to hound and to punish that which is wicked, but to seek and to save that which is lost. His message is not doom, but resurrection.

The Christian view of salvation encompasses the intellectual as well as the moral and spiritual; it is at once personal and social; it is both present and future; it is ancient and modern; it is special, yet all-inclusive. It is the Good News of God in Christ.

Notes

CHAPTER 2

1. *Adventures of Ideas*, p. 221.
2. *Ibid.*, p. 63.
3. *The Meaning of History*, p. 16.

CHAPTER 3

1. *Ephesians* 1:10 (A. V.).
2. C. H. Dodd, *History and the Gospel*, p. 167.
3. *Psalms* 103:7.
4. *Exodus* 3:14.
5. Nicholas Berdyaev, *The Meaning of History*, p. 91.
6. *Mark* 1:15 (A. V.).
7. *Luke* 2:25 (A. V.).
8. *Matthew* 11:12 (The author's translation from the Greek).
9. James Moffatt, *The Thrill of Tradition*, p. 51.
10. *Galatians* 4:4.
11. It is employed with very weighty significance in the speculations of the Gnostics. See the article on "Pleroma" in the *Encyclopedia of Religion and Ethics*, ed. by James Hastings.
12. *Romans* 8:22.
13. *Adventures of Ideas*, p. 137.
14. *I Corinthians* 6:2.
15. Stanley R. Hopper, *The Crisis of Faith*, p. 309.
16. José Ortega y Gasset, *Toward a Philosophy of History*, p. 165.
17. *Colossians* 1:17.

CHAPTER 4

1. *The Apocrypha and Pseudepigrapha of the Old Testament*, II, xi.
2. *The Kingdom of God and the Son of Man*, p. 212.
3. *Op. cit.*, p. 184.
4. Maurice Goguel, *The Life Of Jesus*, p. 576.
5. See especially chapters 44 and 52, *Slavonic Enoch*, for lists of these Beatitudes.
6. Charles Guignebert, *The Jewish World in the Time of Jesus*, p. 246.
7. Rudolph Otto, *op. cit.*, p. 208.
8. Søren Kierkegaard, *Concluding Unscientific Postscript*, p. 410.

9. *Ibid.*, p. 411.
10. *Ibid.*, p. 412.

CHAPTER 5

1. *Acts* 2:24.
2. C. H. Dodd, *History and the Gospel*, p. 109.

CHAPTER 6

1. *The Authority Of The Bible*, p. 226.
2. *Principles of Philosophy*, Part I, Section 51.
3. *Op. cit.*, p. 203.
4. *Proceedings of the Tenth International Congress of Philosophy*, Vol. I, Fasc. 1, p. 368, "The Self as a Structural Function within the World", by Risieri Frondizi.
5. *Der Philosophische Glaube*, p. 60 (Author's trans.).
6. *Either/Or*, Vol. II, p. 211.
7. *Annuaire de la Société Suisse de Philosophie*, Vol. III, 1943, p. 74, "Contribution à l'étude de l'existentialisme," by Georges Rageth. (Author's trans.)
8. *Ibid.*, p. 75.
9. *Ibid.*, p. 85.
10. *Philosophy and Phenomenological Research*, Vol. IX, No. 2 (December 1948) p. 207.
11. *Ibid.*, pp. 205, 206.
12. *The Philosophy of Alfred North Whitehead*, ed. by Paul Arthur Schilpp.

CHAPTER 7

1. *Philosophical Understanding and Religious Truth*, p. 154.
2. Fyodor Dostoievsky, *The Brothers Karamazov*, p. 177.
3. C. S. Lewis, *Beyond Personality*, p. 12.
4. Martin Heidegger, *Existence and Being*, pp. 167 ff.
5. *Ibid.*, p. 330.
6. Gerardus van der Leeuw, *Religion in Essence and Manifestation*, pp. 683, 684.
7. *The Primacy of Faith*, p. 142.
8. *Op. cit.*, p. 154.
9. Robert Browning's "Saul."

CHAPTER 8

1. Emil Brunner, *The Philosophy of Religion*, p. 32.
2. *Ibid.*, p. 34.

3. William Temple, *Nature, Man and God*, p. 317.
4. *Ibid.*, p. 316.
5. *Ibid.*, p. 314.
6. *Ibid.*, p. 322.
7. *Our Knowledge of God*, pp. 36, 37.
8. *The Christian Answer*, ed. by Henry P. Van Dusen, p. 98.
9. *Christ The Lord*, pp. 69, 70.
10. Franz Werfel, *Between Heaven and Earth*, p. 146.
11. Reinhold Niebuhr, *The Nature and Destiny of Man*, I, 126.
12. *Op. cit.*, p. 200.
13. *Op. cit.*, p. 312.
14. John Calvin, *Tracts*, III, 267, "The True Method of Giving Peace to Christendom."
15. Nels F. S. Ferré, *Faith And Reason*, p. 125.
16. *The Philosophy of Alfred North Whitehead*, ed. by Schilpp, p. 493.
17. H. D. Wendland, in *The Kingdom of God and History*, an Oxford Conference Book, p. 147.

CHAPTER 9

1. *The Mysticism of Paul the Apostle*, p. 110.
2. *Ibid.*, p. 112.
3. *Ibid.*, pp. 117, 118.
4. *Adventures of Ideas*, p. 205.

CHAPTER 10

1. *Interpretation: A Journal of Bible and Theology*, July 1949, "The Hope of Salvation", p. 261.
2. Moffatt's translation has it, "trouble not." That of Msgr. R. A. Knox, "fret not." Neither is so poignant as "Be not anxious."
3. Luther's New Testament.
4. These four topics are treated in this order in the four successive chapters of *Romans*, 5-8.
5. H. Wheeler Robinson, *Redemption and Revelation*, p. 232.
6. Sv. Norborg, *Varieties of Christian Experience*, p. 171.
7. *Interpretation: A Journal of Bible and Theology*, July 1949, p. 264.
8. The word health is formed from the Anglo-Saxon *hāl*, which means *whole*. There are ancient Germanic forms which in a modern spelling would approximate *wholth*. See any etymological dictionary.
9. Alfred Adler, *The Neurotic Constitution*, p. ix.
10. *Ibid.*, p. 71.
11. *Ibid.*, p. 83.
12. Karen Horney, *The Neurotic Personality of Our Time*, p. 42.
13. *Ibid.*, p. 47.

14. R. S. Lee, *Freud and Christianity*, p. 169.

15. Transference is the psychological mechanism by which the patient attaches himself emotionally to the therapist. Ordinarily a release from this process, in the latter stages of treatment, is very much to the patient's advantage.

16. *Op. cit.*, p. 171.

17. *How Jesus Heals Our Minds Today*, p. 138.

18. Karl A. Menninger, *Man against Himself*, p. 446.

19. *Ibid.*, p. 449.

20. *Op. cit.*, p. 202.

BIBLIOGRAPHY

Including sources, works quoted, and
suggested volumes for further reading

PHILOSOPHY OF EXISTENCE

Annuaire de la Société Suisse de Philosophie, vol. III, Basel: Verlag für Recht und Gesellschaft, 1943.

BUBER, MARTIN. *Between Man and Man*. New York: The Macmillan Company, 1948.

————. *I and Thou*. New York: Charles Scribner's Sons, 1958.

DOSTOIEVSKY, FYODOR. *The Brothers Karamazov*. New York: Random House, 1933.

————. *The Short Novels*. New York: Dial Press, 1945.

Existence, A New Dimension in Psychiatry and Psychology, edited by Rollo May and others. New York: Basic Books, Inc., 1958.

HEIDEGGER, MARTIN. *Being and Time*. New York: Harper and Brothers, 1962.

————. *Existence and Being*. Chicago: Henry Regnery Company, 1949.

————. *Introduction to Metaphysics*. New Haven: Yale University Press, 1959.

JASPERS, KARL. *Man in the Modern Age*. New York: Henry Holt and Company, 1933.

————. *Nietzsche and Christianity*. Chicago: Henry Regnery Company, 1961.

————. *The Perennial Scope of Philosophy*. New York: Philosophical Library, 1949—which is the translation of the following work quoted by the author.

————. *Der Philosophische Glaube*. Zurich: Artemis-Verlag, 1948.

————. *Reason and Existenz*. New York: Farrar, Straus and Cudahy, 1957.

KIERKEGAARD, SØREN. *Concluding Unscientific Postscript*. Princeton, N.J.: Princeton University Press, 1941.

————. *Either/Or*. Princeton, N.J.: Princeton University Press, 1944.

————. *Philosophical Fragments*. Princeton, N.J.: Princeton University Press, 1962.

203

————. *Training in Christianity*. Princeton, N.J.: Princeton University Press, 1944.

NIETZSCHE, FRIEDRICH. *Beyond Good and Evil*. Chicago: Henry Regnery Company, 1955.

————. *Thus Spake Zarathustra*. Chicago: Henry Regnery Company, 1957.

Proceedings of the Tenth International Congress of Philosophy, Vol. I, fasc. 1, Amsterdam: North-Holland Publishing Company, 1949.

RUITENBECK, H. M. (ed.). *Psychoanalysis and Existential Philosophy*. New York: E. P. Dutton and Company, 1962.

SARTRE, JEAN-PAUL. *Being and Nothingness*. New York: Philosophical Library, 1956.

————. *Existentialism and Humanism*. London: Methuen and Company, 1948.

TILLICH, PAUL. *Theology of Culture*. New York: Oxford University Press, 1959.

PHENOMENOLOGY

HUSSERL, EDMUND. *Ideas: General Introduction to Pure Phenomenology*. London: George Allen and Unwin, Ltd., 1931.

LEEUW, GERARDUS VAN DER. *Religion in Essence and Manifestation*. London: George Allen and Unwin, Ltd., 1938.

SCHELER, MAX. *Man's Place in Nature*. New York: The Noonday Press, 1961.

THÉVENAZ, PIERRE. *What Is Phenomenology?* Chicago: Quadrangle Books, Inc., 1962.

TYMIENIECKA, ANNA-TERESA. *Phenomenology and Science in Contemporary European Thought*. New York: The Noonday Press, 1962.

PHILOSOPHY OF SCIENCE

ALEXANDER, SAMUEL. *Space, Time, and Deity*. London: Macmillan and Company, 1934.

BERGMANN, GUSTAV. *Logic and Reality*. Madison: The University of Wisconsin Press, 1964.

BERGSON, HENRI. *Creative Evolution*. New York: Henry Holt and Company, 1911.

————. *Introduction to Metaphysics*. New York: G. P. Putnam's Sons, 1912.

ČAPEK, MILLIČ. *The Philosophical Impact of Contemporary Physics*. Princeton, N.J.: D. Van Nostrand Company, 1961.

FEIGL, HERBERT, and BRODBECK, MAY. *Readings in the Philosophy of Science.* New York: Appleton-Century-Crofts, Inc., 1953.

FRANK, PHILIPP. *Philosophy of Science.* Englewood Cliffs, N.J.: Prentice-Hall, Inc., 1957.

HEIM, KARL. *Christian Faith and Natural Science.* New York: Harper and Brothers, 1957.

―――. *The Transformation of the Scientific World View.* New York: Harper and Brothers, 1953.

MARGENAU, HENRY. *The Nature of Physical Reality.* New York: McGraw-Hill Book Company, 1950.

NORTHROP, FILMER S. C. (ed.). *Man, Nature and God.* New York: Simon and Schuster, 1962.

PLANCK, MAX. *The Universe in the Light of Modern Physics.* New York: W. W. Norton and Company, 1931.

―――. *Where Is Science Going?* New York: W. W. Norton and Company, 1932.

SCHILPP, PAUL ARTHUR (ed.). *The Philosophy of Alfred North Whitehead.* Evanston and Chicago: Northwestern University Press, 1941.

TEILHARD de CHARDIN, PIERRE. *The Phenomenon of Man.* New York: Harper and Brothers, 1959.

WHITEHEAD, ALFRED NORTH. *Process and Reality.* New York: The Macmillan Company, 1929.

―――. *Science and the Modern World.* New York: The Macmillan Company, 1925.

THEORY OF KNOWLEDGE

BAILLIE, JOHN. *Our Knowledge of God.* London: Oxford University Press, 1939.

CASSIRER, ERNST. *An Essay on Man.* New Haven: Yale University Press, 1944.

―――. *The Philosophy of Symbolic Forms.* 3 vols. New Haven: Yale University Press, 1953.

FERRÉ, NELS F. S. *Faith and Reason.* New York: Harper and Brothers, 1946.

FRANK, ERICH. *Philosophical Understanding and Religious Truth.* London: Oxford University Press, 1945.

KRONER, RICHARD. *The Primacy of Faith.* New York: The Macmillan Company, 1943.

LANGER, SUZANNE K. *Philosophy in a New Key.* Cambridge, Mass.: Harvard University Press, 1942.

PSYCHOLOGY

ADLER, ALFRED. *The Neurotic Constitution.* New York: Dodd, Mead and Company, 1926.

BRILL, A. A. (ed.). *The Basic Writings of Sigmund Freud.* New York: The Modern Library, 1938.

FREUD, SIGMUND. *Introductory Lectures on Psychoanalysis.* 1922.

HORNEY, KAREN. *The Neurotic Personality of Our Time.* New York: W. W. Norton and Company, 1937.

LEE, R. S. *Freud and Christianity.* New York: A. A. Wyn, Inc., 1949.

MENNINGER, KARL A. *Man against Himself.* New York: Harcourt, Brace and Company, 1938.

SEABURY, DAVID. *How Jesus Heals Our Minds Today.* Boston: Little, Brown and Company, 1948.

BIBLICAL STUDIES

BORNKAMM, GUNTHER. *Jesus of Nazareth.* New York: Harper and Brothers, 1960.

BULTMANN, RUDOLPH and KUNDSIN, KARL. *Form Criticism.* New York: Harper and Brothers, 1962.

BULTMANN, RUDOLPH. *Jesus Christ and Mythology.* New York: Charles Scribner's Sons, 1958.

————. *Kerygma and Myth.* New York: Harper and Brothers, 1961.

————. *Primitive Christianity in Its Contemporary Setting.* Cleveland: World Publishing Company, 1956.

CHARLES, R. H. *The Apocrypha and Pseudepigrapha of the Old Testament.* Oxford: The Clarendon Press, 1913.

DODD, CHARLES HAROLD. *The Authority of the Bible.* London: Nisbet and Company, 1947.

————. *History and the Gospel.* New York: Charles Scribner's Sons, 1938.

EICHRODT, WALTER. *Theology of the Old Testament.* (Vol. I) Philadelphia: Westminster Press, 1961.

GOGUEL, MAURICE. *The Life of Jesus.* New York: The Macmillan Company, 1933.

GUIGNEBERT, CHARLES. *The Jewish World in the Time of Jesus.* New York: E. P. Dutton and Company, 1939.

MOFFATT, JAMES. *The Thrill of Tradition.* New York: The Macmillan Company, 1944.

OGDEN, SCHUBERT N. *Christ Without Myth.* New York: Harper and Brothers, 1961.

OTTO, RUDOLPH. *The Kingdom of God and the Son of Man.* London: Lutterworth Press, 1943.

RAD, GERHARD VON. *Old Testament Theology.* New York: Harper and Brothers, 1962.

ROBINSON, H. WHEELER. *Redemption and Revelation.* London: Nisbet and Company, Ltd., 1942.

ROBINSON, JAMES M. *The New Quest of the Historical Jesus.* Naperville, Ill.: Allenson, 1959.

ROWLEY, HAROLD HENRY. *The Relevance of Apocalyptic.* London: Lutterworth Press, 1944.

SANTAYANA, GEORGE. *The Idea of Christ in the Gospels.* New York: Charles Scribner's Sons, 1946.

SCHWEITZER, ALBERT. *The Mysticism of Paul the Apostle.* New York: Henry Holt and Company, 1931.

————. *The Quest of the Historical Jesus.* New York: The Macmillan Company.

WRIGHT, GEORGE ERNEST. *The Challenge of Israel's Faith.* Chicago: The University of Chicago Press, 1944.

RELIGION

BRUNNER, HEINRICH EMIL. *The Philosophy of Religion.* New York: Charles Scribner's Sons, 1937.

CALVIN, JOHN. *Tracts* (Vol. III) Edinburgh: The Calvin Translation Society, 1851.

HEIM, KARL. *God Transcendent.* London: Nisbet and Company, Ltd., 1935.

HOPPER, STANLEY R. *The Crisis of Faith.* New York and Nashville: Abingdon-Cokesbury, 1944.

KNOX, JOHN. *Christ the Lord.* Chicago: Willett, Clark and Company, 1945.

LEWIS, C. S. *Beyond Personality.* New York: The Macmillan Company, 1945.

NIEBUHR, REINHOLD. *The Nature and Destiny of Man.* New York: Charles Scribner's Sons, 1941.

NORBORG, SV. *Varieties of Christian Experience.* Minneapolis: Augsburg Publishing House, 1937.

TEMPLE, WILLIAM. *Nature, Man, and God.* London: Macmillan and Company, 1934.

TILLICH, PAUL. *Dynamics of Faith.* New York: Harper and Brothers, 1957.

———. *Systematic Theology.* Chicago: University of Chicago Press. Three volumes. 1951, 1957, 1963.

VAN DUSEN, HENRY P. *The Christian Answer.* New York: Charles Scribner's Sons, 1945.

WERFEL, FRANZ. *Between Heaven and Earth.* New York: Philosophical Library, 1944.

PHILOSOPHY OF HISTORY

BERDYAEV, NICOLAS. *The Meaning of History.* New York: Charles Scribner's Sons, 1936.

BULTMANN, RUDOLPH. *History and Eschatology.* New York: Harper and Brothers, 1962.

CULLMANN, OSCAR. *Christ and Time.* Philadelphia: Westminster Press, 1950.

DILTHEY, WILHELM. *Pattern and Meaning in History.* New York: Harper and Brothers, 1962.

———. *Théorie des Conceptions du Monde.* Paris: Presses Universitaires de France, 1946. (Translation by Louis Sauzin of Dilthey's *Weltanschauungslehre*).

The Kingdom of God and History. An Oxford Conference Book, Chicago: Willett, Clark and Company, 1938.

LÖWITH, KARL. *Meaning in History.* Chicago: The University of Chicago Press, 1949.

NORTHROP, FILMER S. C. *The Meeting of East and West.* New York: The Macmillan Company, 1946.

ORTEGA Y GASSET, JOSÉ. *Toward a Philosophy of History.* New York: W. W. Norton and Company, 1941.

TILLICH, PAUL. *The Interpretation of History.* New York: Charles Scribner's Sons, 1936.

WHITEHEAD, ALFRED NORTH. *Adventures of Ideas.* New York: The Macmillan Company, 1940.

GENERAL INDEX

Abbagnano, Nicola, 110-112
Abraham, 39, 78
actualization (messianic role), 98, 99 f.
Adams, Henry, 135
Adler, Alfred, 189
Amos, 177
analytical psychology, 13
angle of elevation, 49, 130 f.
anxiety, 106, 180 f., 188 ff., 192, 198
apocryphal writings. *See* Pseude-pigraphal writings
archaic structures, 9, 29 f.
Aristotle, 12
ascension of Christ, the, 93 f.
atonement, the, 88 ff.
Augustine, St., 32
authority, 120 f., 140, 153 f., 161 f.

Bahá'í, 7
Baillie, John, 141
Barth, Karl, 140, 142 f., 166, 171
becoming, 118 f.
being, 15, 25 ff., 197 f.; final form of, 110; of Christ and God, 112, 114-119; of man, 107 f.; as product of choice, 25 f., 108-114
Berdyaev, Nicolas, 28, 43 f.
Bergson, Henri, 13, 21 f., 168
Bible, the, 130-132, Chapter. VIII, 161-165
bifurcation of nature, 29
Binswanger, Ludwig, 190

Bixler, J. S., 113
boundary-situations, 27
bridge-facts, 86-94
Browning, Robert, 137 (footnote)
Brunner, H. Emil, 140, 171
Buddhism, 35
Bultmann, Rudolph, 94 f.

Calvin, John, 154, 168, 170 f.
canon of Scripture, the, 152-156, 163 f.
care, 180
Carthage, Council of, 153
Cassirer, Ernst, 24 f., 101
categories of the organismic world-view, 32 ff.
centrality of the Christian event, 39 f., 48 f., 55 ff., 102
Charles, R. H., 58-61
Christ, 11 f., 35 ff., 46 ff., 50 f., 68, 72-81, 178-180, 182, 192, 198
Christology, existential, 95, Chapter VI
Church, the, 2-8, 50 f., 85, 106, Chapter IX
coherent perspective, 51 f.
Communism, 2 f., 34, 54
completion and projection (messianic role), 98, 100-102, 112 ff.
comprehensiveness, 33 ff.
concretion, 17, 31, 49
Confucius, 35
continuum, 31; irregular bounded, 130

209